Basic skills in geography

geography

Book 1

David Rose

OXFORD UNIVERSITY PRESS 1988

For the teacher

- *Basic Skills in Geography* deals with key geographical concepts by emphasizing skills.
- The course stresses an individualized activities-based approach to learning by highlighting graphic work.
- The scheme incorporates a diagnostic element.
- Book 1 teaches children about the structure of their immediate environment and highlights the geography of the British Isles.

Using the book

This book is divided into eleven units. Each unit deals with a key geographical concept or a particular skill, and develops it sequentially, over a series of well-structured stages.

The **key words** which head each section are important reference points which guide the pupil through the content of each unit. They can be reinforced by the teacher in subsequent follow-up activities.

The **exercises** are graded, allowing all pupils the opportunity to achieve a degree of success. There are five types of specific exercise, which appear in the early part of each unit. This allows a pattern of work to become easily established, enabling all pupils to develop a level of independence in their work. More open-ended questions appear at the end of the units. As pupils become more confident and experience success, they will eventually proceed to these more demanding exercises.

Some of the tasks within each unit contain a **diagnostic** element, in order to indicate a specific weakness in the skill being covered. It should be clear to the teacher at what stage a particular weakness appears. Remedial action can then be taken, as part of a pupil's learning programme. In a mixed ability setting this book can be used by the geography specialist to develop a child's geographical skills. Once a satisfactory skill level has been established the pupil can progress to the next level, where basic skills may be assumed.

For Andrew, Stuart and Laura

Oxford University Press, Walton Street, Oxford OX2 6DP

Oxford New York Toronto
Delhi Bombay Calcutta Madras Karachi
Petaling Jaya Singapore Hong Kong Tokyo
Nairobi Dar es Salaam Cape Town
Melbourne Auckland
and associated companies in
Beirut Berlin Ibadan Nicosia

Oxford is a trade mark of Oxford University Press

© Oxford University Press 1988
ISBN 0 19 83338 2

Typeset by Oxprint Limited
Printed in Hong Kong

Contents

How to do the work

This section shows you how to answer the questions in this book.

First look at these photographs:

Photograph 1

Photograph 2

There are five main types of questions in this book. They are:

Type 1: True or false

If you think a sentence is correct, write *true* .
If you do not think it is correct, write *false* .

This type of exercise is shown by this sign **T/F**

T/F   **Exercise A**

Look at Photograph 1. Write *true* or *false* for the sentences below. Answer like this: *1. true*

1. The photograph shows the countryside.
2. The photograph shows farmland.
3. There are no roads in the photograph.
4. There is woodland in the photograph.
5. There is a big city in the photograph.
6. There is a farm in the photograph.

Type 2: Make your choice

In this type of question, you have to choose the correct answer. Only one of the answers is correct. You must copy the sentence so that it is correct.

This type of exercise is shown by this sign **CH**

Type 3: Matching

In this type of exercise you have to put together the two parts of a sentence, to make a complete sentence.
Sometimes you may only have to match letters and words.

This type of exercise is shown by this sign **M**

Type 4: Fill in the gaps

In this type of exercise you have to copy the sentences and put in the missing words, so it all makes sense. Sometimes you are given a list of words to choose from.

This type of exercise is shown by this sign **FG**

Type 5: Finish the sentence

In this type of exercise you have to copy the sentence which is not finished. You must finish the sentence on your own.

This type of exercise is shown by this sign **FS**

There are other types of exercises. Some have no sign.
If they have the sign **T** see your teacher first.

CH Exercise B

Look at Photograph 2. Copy and complete the sentences below. Answer like this:

1. Photograph 2 shows a city.

1. Photograph 2 shows a (farm / village / city).
2. This city has many (tall / low / short) buildings.
3. This city covers a lot of (sea / land / marsh).
4. This city has a lot of (houses / farms / fields).
5. There are (no / many / few) roads in this city.

M Exercise C

Match the words below with their sentence endings. Answer like this:

1. People live in towns and in the country.

Cities / People / Farms / Country

1. _____ live in towns and in the country.
2. _____ have more people than the countryside.
3. _____ areas usually have farms.
4. _____ are not usually found in cities.

FG Exercise D

Copy and complete the sentences below.

The two photographs of Britain are _____ different. Britain is a land _____ differences. Some parts are very _____ and crowded. These places have _____ of towns and cities. Other _____ have open farmland, and lots of _____ countryside. Britain has many beautiful _____.

FS Exercise E

Copy and complete the sentences below.

1. The roads in Photograph 2 _____
2. The farms in Photograph 1 _____
3. The buildings in Photograph 2 _____
4. The roads in Photograph 1 _____

Exercise F

1. Write a sentence about Photograph 1.
2. Write a sentence about Photograph 2.
3. Write a sentence about where you live.

Shapes 1

Key words

circle   regular
triangle   irregular
square   rectangle

This section is about different shapes.

FG   **Exercise A**

Look at these shapes.

Two of the shapes are the same. Which two are the same? Answer like this:

1. The two shapes which are the same are A and D.

Do the rest on your own. Copy and complete the sentence each time and draw the shapes.

2. The two shapes which are the same are _____ and _____.

 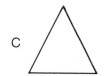

3. The two shapes which are the same are _____ and _____.

4. The two shapes which are the same are _____ and _____.

5. The two shapes which are the same are _____ and _____.

FS   **Exercise B**

This is a circle.

This is a triangle.

This is a square

This is a rectangle.

So is this.

Look at your answers again. Write them out again, like this:

1. The two shapes are both ___*circles*___.
2. The two shapes are both _____.
3. The two shapes are both _____.
4. The two shapes are both _____.
5. The two shapes are both _____.

Exercise C

Find the two shapes which are exactly the same.

1. The two shapes which are the same are _____ and _____.

A   B   C   D

2. The two shapes which are the same are _____ and _____.

A   B   C   D

3. The two shapes which are the same are _____ and _____.

A   B   C   D

4. The two shapes which are the same are _____ and _____.

A   B   C   D

5. The two shapes which are the same are _____ and _____.

A   B   C   D

Circles, triangles and rectangles are regular shapes. Shapes which are not regular are called irregular shapes.

M **Exercise D**

Match the two irregular shapes.

1. The two matching irregular shapes are _____ and _____.

2. The two matching irregular shapes are _____ and _____.

3. The two matching irregular shapes are _____ and _____.

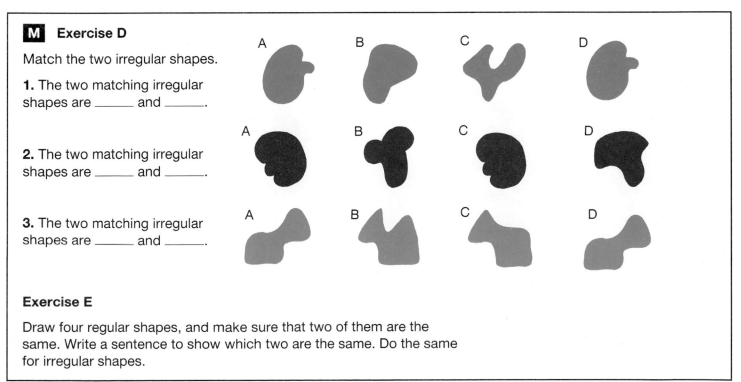

Exercise E

Draw four regular shapes, and make sure that two of them are the same. Write a sentence to show which two are the same. Do the same for irregular shapes.

Shapes 2

This section is about the shapes of countries and continents.

M **Exercise A**

Find the two shapes which are the same and complete the sentences.

1. The two matching shapes are _____ and _____.

A  B C D E

2. The two matching shapes are _____ and _____.

A 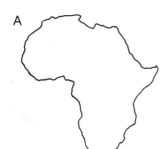 B  C  D

3. The two matching shapes are _____ and _____.

A  B  C  D

4. The two matching shapes are _____ and _____.

A  B  C  D

5. The two matching shapes are _____ and _____.

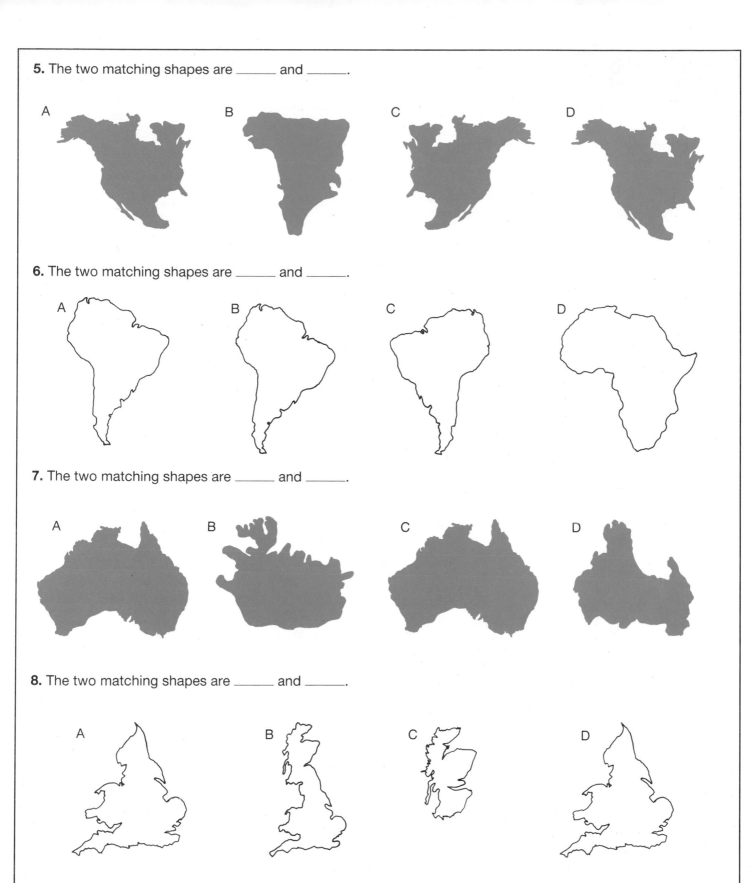

A   B   C   D

6. The two matching shapes are _____ and _____.

A   B   C   D

7. The two matching shapes are _____ and _____.

A   B   C   D

8. The two matching shapes are _____ and _____.

A   B   C   D

Exercise B

Choose any two of the questions from Exercise A. Copy the matching
shapes from each question.

Shapes 3

This section is about the shapes of places in the British Isles.

Look at Figure 1. It shows the shapes of England, Scotland, Wales, Northern Ireland and the Republic of Ireland.

This is the shape of **Scotland**.

This is the shape of **Northern Ireland**.

This is the shape of the **Republic of Ireland**.

This is the shape of **England**.

This is the shape of **Wales**.

Figure 1

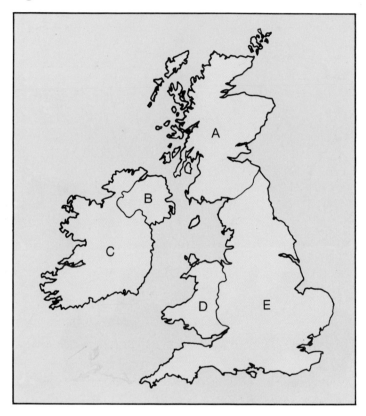

FS Exercise A

Copy and complete these sentences.

1. Shape A is called _____.
2. Shape B is called _____.
3. Shape C is called _____.
4. Shape D is called _____.
5. Shape E is called _____.

T Exercise B

Trace these shapes.

1. England   **4.** Northern Ireland
2. Scotland   **5.** Republic of Ireland
3. Wales

T/F Exercise C

Copy these sentences and then write *true* or *false* after them (this has already been done for the first sentence).

1. England is larger than Wales. *true*
2. England is larger than Scotland.
3. The Republic of Ireland is smaller than Northern Ireland.
4. Wales is larger than Northern Ireland.
5. England and Wales are larger than Northern Ireland and the Republic of Ireland.
6. Wales is joined to England.
7. Scotland is joined to Northern Ireland.
8. Scotland and Wales are both joined to England.

Figure 2

Figure 3

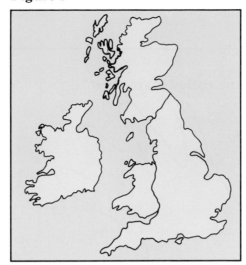

FS Exercise D

Look at Figures 2–5. Each is like Figure 1, but a shape is missing. Name the missing shape.

1. In Figure 2 the missing shape is _____.
2. In Figure 3 the missing shape is _____.
3. In Figure 4 the missing shape is _____.
4. In Figure 5 the missing shape is _____.
5. In Figure 6 the missing shape is _____.

Figure 4

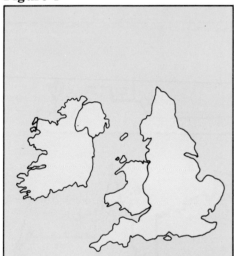

Figure 5

Figure 6

Figure 7

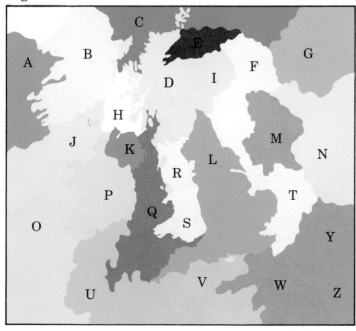

FS Exercise E

The shapes of England, Scotland, Wales, Northern Ireland, and the Republic of Ireland are hidden in Figure 7. Find them. Then copy and complete the sentences.

1. Scotland is shape _____.
2. The Republic of Ireland is shape _____.
3. Northern Ireland is shape _____.
4. Wales is shape _____.
5. England is shape _____.

T Exercise F

1. Trace the shapes of England, Scotland, Wales, Northern Ireland and the Republic of Ireland on to separate sheets of paper.
2. Cut out the shapes.
3. Put them together so they look like Figure 1.

Shapes 4

This section is about a special shape called an outline.

Place your hand on a piece of paper. Draw around your hand with a pencil. Like this:

Now take your hand off the paper. You have made a drawing of your hand. This drawing is called an outline.

M **Exercise A**

Match the outlines below with these words:
boat / car / horse / train / church / castle

Answer like this: *1. car*

1.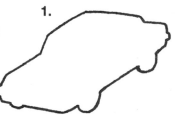

2.

3.    4.   5.    6.

Exercise B

Draw your own outline shapes for the following:

1. A bottle   **2.** A house   **3.** An aeroplane   **4.** A lorry

M **Exercise C**

Name the two matching outlines by copying and completing the sentences below.

A   B   C    A  B  C

1. The two matching outlines are _____ and _____.   **2.** The two matching outlines are _____ and _____.

Figure 1

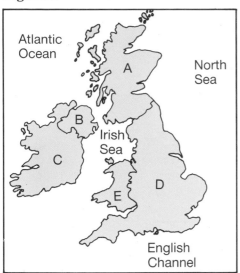

Look at these outlines:

This is Northern Ireland

This is the Republic of Ireland

This is Scotland

This is Wales

This is England

Figure 2

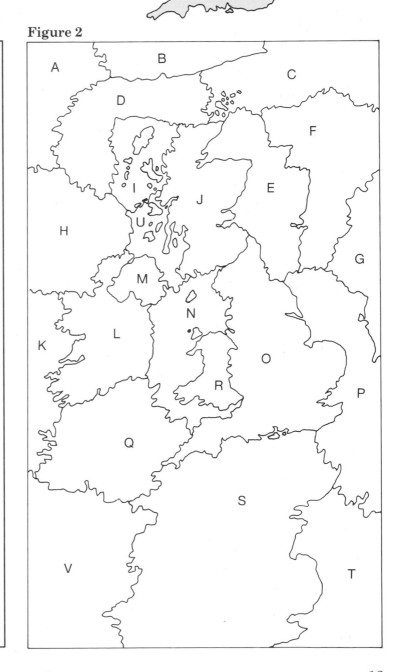

FS **Exercise C**

Look at Figure 1 above.
Copy and complete these sentences:

1. Outline A is called _____.
2. Outline B is called _____.
3. Outline C is called _____.
4. Outline D is called _____.
5. Outline E is called _____.

T **Exercise D**

On an outline of the British Isles, print the names of these countries in the correct places:
England / Scotland / Wales
Northern Ireland / Republic of Ireland

Exercise E

On your outline, print the names of these seas in the correct places:
North Sea / Irish Sea
English Channel / Atlantic Ocean

FS **Exercise F**

Look at Figure 2. The outlines of England, Scotland, Wales, Northern Ireland and the Republic of Ireland are hidden. Can you find them?
Answer like this:

1. Scotland is outline __J__.
2. The Republic of Ireland is outline _____.
3. Northern Ireland is outline _____.
4. Wales is outline _____.
5. England is outline _____.

Plans 1

This section is about things seen from above.

Look at this drawing of a table:

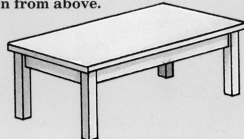

The table looks different when it is seen from above.
When you look down on the table, it will look like this:

This is a tin of soup:    This is the same tin of soup seen from above:

A drawing of something seen from above is called a plan.

M   **Exercise A**

Look at these drawings and the plans below.

Match the drawings and the plans. Write your
answers like this: *1. car = D*

1. car   **2.** chair   **3.** television   **4.** boy   **5.** house

     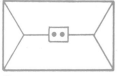   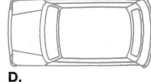   

A.   **B.**   **C.**   **D.**   **E.**

Exercise B

Copy one of the drawings above. Draw its plan.

Exercise C

Draw something you can see in the classroom. Make
a plan of what you have drawn.

M Exercise D

Match the letters on the drawing with the words below.

Answer like this:

A = settee

door / window / settee / chair / table / fireplace / television / sideboard

M Exercise E

Look at the plan of the room.

Match the letters on the plan with the words below.

Answer like this:

A = table

door / window / settee / chair / table / fireplace / television / sideboard

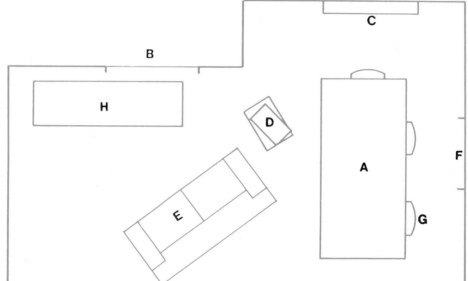

M Exercise F

Look at the plan of the house and the land outside. Match the letters on the plan with the words below.

Answer like this:

A = bus

fence / bus / tree / chimney / car / post box / telephone box / path

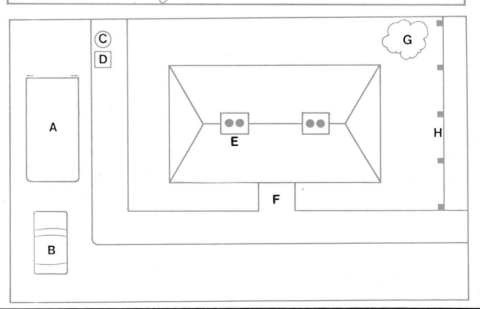

Plans 2

This section is about a plan of a street.

Look at this photograph of a
housing estate:

This is a street plan of the same
housing estate. Look at the plan.
Some of the street names have
been put on the plan.

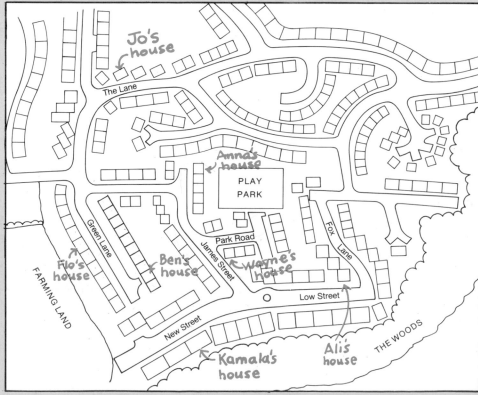

A group of friends live on this housing estate. Their names are Ben, Flo, Kamala, Jo, Wayne, Anna and Ali. Find where they live by looking at the plan.

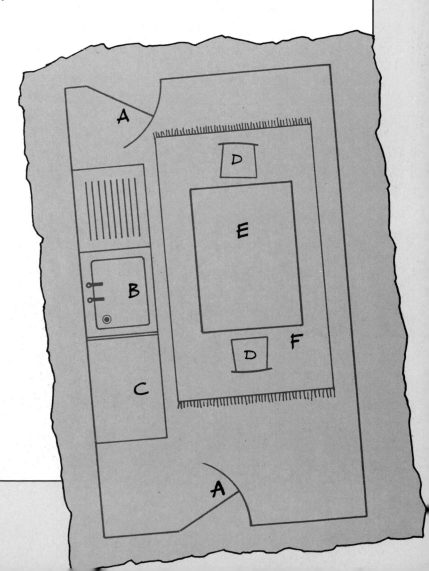

FG **Exercise A**

Copy and complete these sentences:

1. Kamala lives in _____ Street.
2. Jo lives in The _____.
3. Ben and Flo live in _____ Lane.
4. The woods are behind _____ Street and _____ Street.
5. Ali's house is near the corner of Low Street and _____ Lane.
6. Wayne's house is at the corner of Park Road and _____ Street.
7. There are _____ houses on Flo's side of Green Lane.
8. There are _____ houses on Ben's side of Green Lane.

CH **Exercise B**

There is a party at Anna's house. Kamala and Ali are going to call for Wayne first. Copy these sentences to show how they got to the party:

Kamala left her house and walked along (New / Low) Street. At the end of the street Kamala turned (left / right). She walked along (James / Low) Street towards Wayne's house. Ali left home a bit later. He turned right and walked along (Low Street / Fox Lane) towards Wayne's house.

Exercise C

Ben and Flo are also going to the party. They are going to meet at Jo's house, first.

Write some sentences to show how they all got to the party at Anna's house.

M **Exercise D**

This is a plan of Anna's kitchen. Match the letters on the plan with things from the list. Answer like this:

A = doors

chairs / doors / table / carpet / sink / cupboard

Exercise E

Draw a plan of any room in your home. Put things like chairs, tables and doors on your plan.

Exercise F

1. Write down two things that you will not see on a plan.
2. Why do you think these two things are not shown on a plan?

Maps 1

This section is about maps. A map is a plan of a place.

Look at the photograph below. It shows what this country looks like from space. Beside the photograph is a map of the British Isles.

A map is like a plan. Both try to show what things look like from above.

The map shows many islands. There are two large ones and lots of smaller ones. The largest island is called Great Britain and is divided into three parts. Each part is called a country. The three countries are England, Scotland and Wales.

Photograph: The British Isles from a space satellite

T/F Exercise A

Copy these sentences and then write *true* or *false* after each one.

1. A plan shows what things look like from above.
2. A photograph shows more than a plan.
3. A plan leaves some things out.
4. A photograph is always taken from the ground.
5. A map is like a plan.

FG Exercise B

Copy and complete these sentences, using words from the list below:

A map is like a _____. A plan and a _____ try to show the _____ from above. A _____ can also do this. _____ photographs are taken from _____.

world / plan / space / photograph / map / satellite

The other large island is called Ireland. It is now divided into two countries: Northern Ireland and the Republic of Ireland.

So there are five countries in the British Isles: England, Scotland, Wales, Northern Ireland and the Republic of Ireland.

The United Kingdom (U.K. for short) is made up of England, Scotland, Wales and Northern Ireland.

The Republic of Ireland is a separate country with its own government.

Map The British Isles

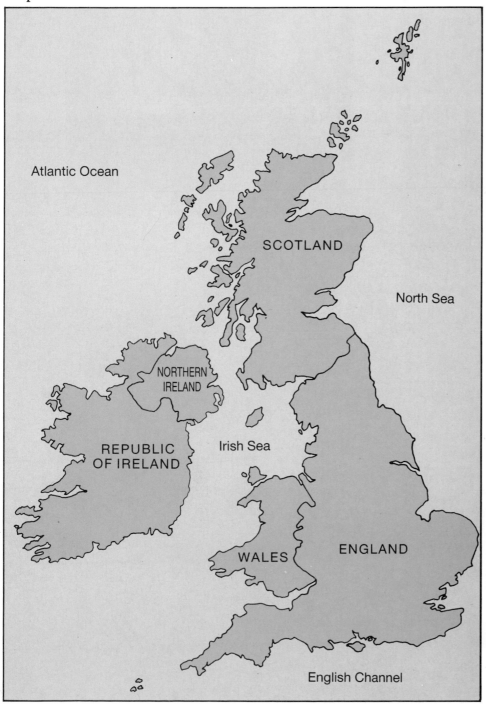

Copy and complete this:

The map shows many _____. There are two large ones _____ lots of smaller ones. The _____ island is divided into three _____. Each part is called a _____. The three countries are England, _____ and Wales. Ireland is divided into two _____.The two countries are called _____ Ireland and the Republic of _____.

Exercise D

These are the flags of the different countries. Copy them.

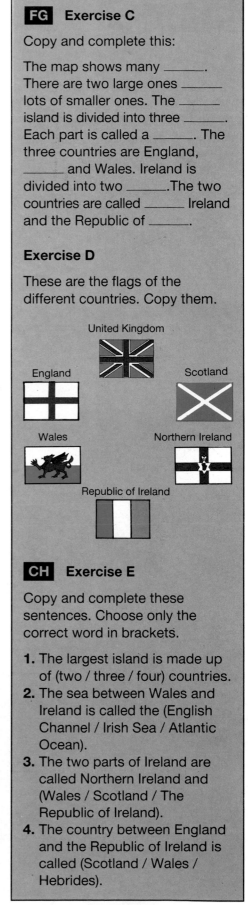

CH **Exercise E**

Copy and complete these sentences. Choose only the correct word in brackets.

1. The largest island is made up of (two / three / four) countries.
2. The sea between Wales and Ireland is called the (English Channel / Irish Sea / Atlantic Ocean).
3. The two parts of Ireland are called Northern Ireland and (Wales / Scotland / The Republic of Ireland).
4. The country between England and the Republic of Ireland is called (Scotland / Wales / Hebrides).

Maps 2

This section is about maps of the British Isles and the World.

This photograph from space shows the British Isles and part of Europe.

The map below shows more than the photograph. It is a map of the world. All of the world cannot be shown on one photograph. The world is round, so part of it is always out of sight, from space.
The map shows the whole world as if spread out on flat paper.

Photograph 1 The British Isles and Europe from space

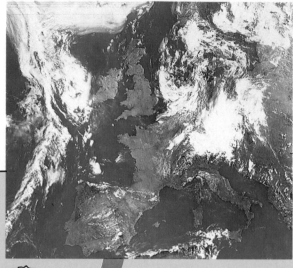

Map The World

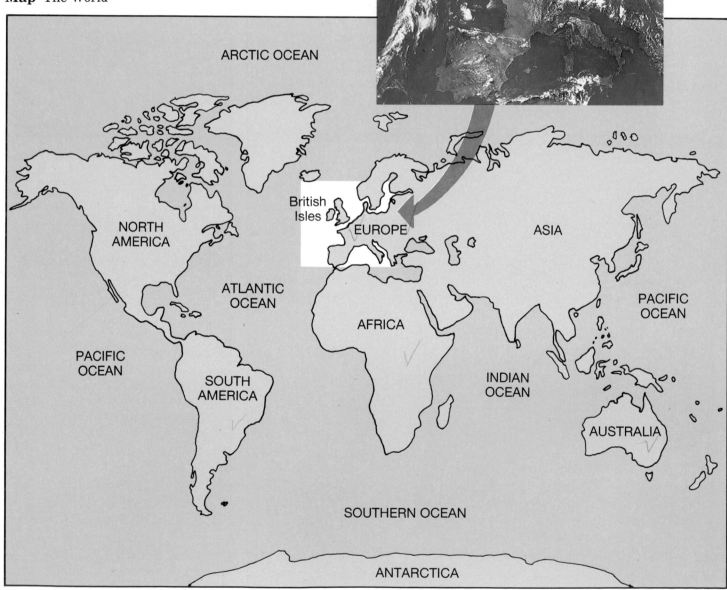

The British Isles are only a very small part of the world's land surface. The countries of the British Isles are smaller than many other countries.

Most of the surface of the world is water. Less than a third of the world's surface is land. The largest areas of land are called continents. There are seven continents: Europe, Asia, Africa, North America, South America, Australia, and Antarctica.

The photographs below show two of the continents.

Photograph 2

Photograph 3

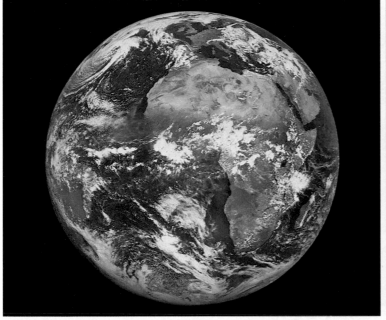

CH Exercise C

Copy and complete the sentences below.

1. Most of the world's surface is (land / water).
2. The countries of the British Isles are (small / large).
3. The largest areas of land are called (countries / continents).
4. The British Isles are part of (Europe / North America).
5. Large areas of water are called (continents / oceans).

FS Exercise D

Look at the map, and then copy and complete the sentences below:

1. The Atlantic Ocean is between the British Isles and _____ _____.
2. The Indian Ocean is between _____ and _____.
3. Asia and North America are separated by the _____ _____.

CH Exercise E

Look at the two photographs above, and then copy and complete these sentences:

1. Photograph 2 shows the continent called (Africa / Australia / South America).
2. Photograph 3 shows the continent called (North America / Australia / Europe).

Exercise F

Name the four continents *not* shown in the photographs on these pages.

Exercise G

Name two things you can see in the photographs above that are not shown on the map.

Photographs 1

Key words

village   population
town   countryside
city

This section is about where people live in Britain.

Look at the photographs on these two pages very carefully. Only by looking carefully will you see important things. There are some questions on the next page to help you look.

People in Britain live in different kinds of places. Some people live in small places called villages.

This is a village.

Photograph 1 A village

Some people live in bigger places called towns. More people live in towns than in villages. There are more jobs in a town than in a village.

This is a town.

Photograph 2 A town

The biggest places are called cities. A city is a big town. It often has a cathedral.

This is a city.

Photograph 3 A city

Most people in Britain live in a village or a town or a city. Some live on farms or houses in the countryside. All the people make up Britain's **population**.

T/F Exercise A

Write true or false for each question.
Answer like this: *1. true*

Photograph 1 A village

1. The village has narrow roads.
2. The village has a church.
3. The village has many tall buildings.
4. The village is in a farming area.
5. There is one main road through the village.
6. This village is near some woods.
7. The village has many shops.
8. The church is near a stream.

Photograph 2 A town

1. The town is beside a river.
2. The town has a bus station.
3. The town is built on flat land.
4. The town has a bridge.
5. The town has more than one factory.
6. All the buildings are houses.
7. This town has one car park.
8. The factories are on the edge of town.
9. There are no zebra road crossings in this town.
10. The photograph was taken in summer.

Photograph 3 A city

1. The city is beside a river.
2. There is a bridge across the river.
3. This city has a cathedral.
4. Most of the buildings in the city centre are tall.
5. This city has no trees.
6. Most of the buildings in the centre are very old.
7. There are docks on the river.
8. All the roads have two lanes.
9. There are boats on the river.
10. There is plenty of green space in the city.

Exercise B

Write two sentences of your own about each photograph.

Exercise C

1. Write down two good things about living in a village.
2. Write down two good things about living in towns and cities.

Exercise D

1. Write down two bad things about living in a village.
2. Write down two bad things about living in towns and cities.

Exercise E

Copy and complete this sentence:
I would like to live in a (village / town / city) because

_____.

T Exercise F

Collect photographs of your own village, town or city. You could cut them out of local newspapers. Paste them into your book. Then write some sentences about what the photographs show.

Exercise G

Look at the photographs of the village, town and city. Use some of your answers from Exercise A to help you, and write down the main differences between a village, a town and a city.

Photographs 2

Key words

aerial   prosperous
housing   declining

This section is about different kinds of villages.

Look at this photograph of a
village. The photograph was
taken from an aeroplane. It is
called an aerial photograph.

Photograph 1

M **Exercise A**

Find the letters A to E on Photograph 1. Match the
letters on the photograph with the sentence endings
below.
Answer like this:

1. __C__ is the village church.
2. _____ is the new road.
3. _____ is the old road.
4. _____ is the village school.
5. _____ is the market place.

Exercise B

Write five sentences about what you can see in
Photograph 1.

CH **Exercise C**

Copy and complete the sentences below:

1. The largest building is the (school / church / shop).
2. The market place is at the (centre / edge / outside)
   of the village.
3. The new road takes traffic (inside / around / above)
   the village.
4. This village looks very (quiet / noisy / busy).

Exercise D

Do you think the school is a primary school or a
secondary school? Write down how you know.

This is an aerial photograph of a different kind of village. It was built around a coal mine.

Photograph 2

page 25

M **Exercise E**

Look at the photograph above. Match the letters on the photograph with the sentence endings below:

1. _____ is the coal mine.
2. _____ is the slag heap.
3. _____ is a playground.
4. _____ is a road.
5. _____ is a railway.

Exercise F

1. Write down three things you can see in Photograph 1 that are not in Photograph 2.
2. Write down three things you can see in Photograph 2 that are not in Photograph 1.

Exercise G

1. Use a dictionary to write down the meanings of the following words:
   rural / industrial / bleak / prosperous
2. Write a sentence for each of the words to show how it describes either Photograph 1 or Photograph 2.

Exercise H

Which of these two villages would you rather live in? Write three sentences or more to explain your answer.

Exercise I

Make a list of all of the villages near you. Beside each village name write 1, 2 or 3:
1 means it is a village like Photograph 1.
2 means it is a village like Photograph 2.
3 means it is not like either Photograph 1 or Photograph 2.

Photographs 3

This section is about different kinds of towns.

Look at the photograph below. It is an aerial photograph of Blackpool. Lots of people go to Blackpool for their holidays, so it is a very busy place in summer. Blackpool is a seaside resort.

Photograph 1 Blackpool from the air

M **Exercise A**

Look at the photograph of Blackpool. Match the letters on the photograph with the sentence endings below. Answer like this:

1. _C_ is Blackpool tower.
2. _____ is the promenade.
3. _____ is the railway station.
4. _____ is the beach.
5. _____ is a pier.

Exercise B

If you think the things listed below are in the photograph write _yes_. If you do not think they are, write _no_.

Answer like this: 1. _Yes_

1. A pier
2. A hotel
3. A park
4. A boat
5. A coach park
6. A car park
7. A swimming pool
8. A coal mine
9. An office
10. An amusement centre

Exercise C

1. Write down three good things about living in a seaside resort.
2. Write down three bad things about living in a seaside resort.

Exercise D

1. Draw a poster to show why Blackpool is a good town to visit.
2. Draw a poster for your own town to show the good things in it.

Look at this photograph of Swindon. It is a different kind of town. Swindon has lots of factories and offices. It is an industrial town and is busy all the year round.

Photograph 2 Swindon from the air

M **Exercise E**

Look at the photograph of Swindon. Match the letters on the photograph with the words below:

1. _____ is a bus station.
2. _____ is a housing area.
3. _____ is a tall office block.
4. _____ is a railway depot.
5. _____ is a car park.

Exercise G

1. Look at both photographs and write down **three** things that both towns have.
2. Write down **three** things you can see in Blackpool, but not in Swindon.
3. Write down **three** things you can see in Swindon that you will see in most towns.

Exercise F

Look at these drawings and copy and complete the sentences below:

1. Drawing 1 shows a (modern / old) building.
2. Drawing 2 shows a (modern / old) building.
3. Swindon has lots of (modern / old) buildings.

Exercise H

1. Describe how your town is different from Swindon or Blackpool.
2. Describe how your town is like lots of other towns in Britain.

Sketches 1

This section is about drawing places. A simple drawing of a place is called a sketch.

Look at this house. It is on its own. A house which is on its own is called a detached house.

This drawing is a sketch of the same detached house.

Photograph 1 Detached house

Photograph 2 Semi-detached houses

These are semi-detached houses. They are joined to each other on one side only.

Photograph 3 Terraced houses

Houses attached on both sides and built in a long row are called terraced houses.

Photograph 4 Flats

There are other kinds of houses. Flats are like a lot of houses built together in one block. The block can be two, three or more storeys high.

Drawing a sketch

This is how to draw a sketch from a photograph:

1. Draw a box the same size as the photograph. Mark it into four parts, like this:

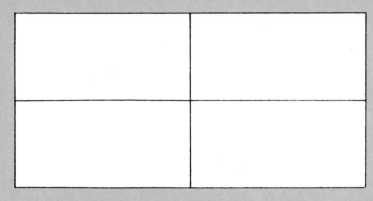

2. Draw in the most important outlines. Use the small boxes to help you, like this:

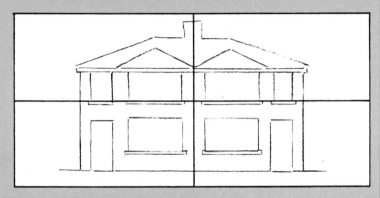

3. Draw in more lines. Leave out things which are not important.

FG **Exercise A**

Copy and complete these sentences:

1. A house on its own is called a _____ house.
2. Two houses joined to each other on one side are called _____ _____ houses.
3. Houses joined together on both sides are called _____ houses.
4. Homes built on top of each other are called _____ .

Exercise B

Look at the photograph of the flats. The unfinished sketch below is of the flats. Copy and complete the sketch on your own.

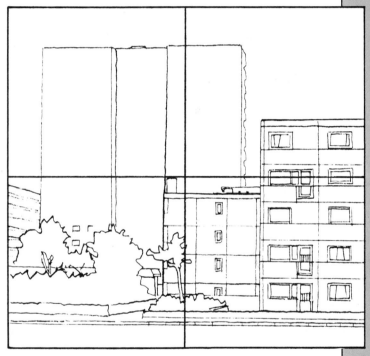

Exercise C

Look at the photograph of the terraced houses. Draw a sketch of them.

Exercise D

Draw a sketch of your own house or flat.

FS **Exercise E**

Copy and complete the sentences below. (Use a dictionary to help you)

1. A bungalow is _____
2. A maisonette is _____

Sketches 2

This section is about drawing a sketch.

A group of friends wanted to draw a sketch. They went to a street in the centre of town. This is the street:

Photograph 1
A street in the centre of town

This is their sketch of the street.

Exercise A

Copy the sketch and make it the same size.

Exercise B

Use the photograph to help you, and draw more things on to your sketch. (Do not draw cars or people)

Exercise C

Write four sentences about the street you have drawn.

Exercise D

Draw a sketch of a street near your school.

This is an aerial photograph of Doncaster.

Building A is a church. This is a sketch of the church.

Building B is a bus depot and car park. This is a sketch of the car park.

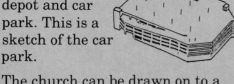

The church can be drawn on to a sketch as shown below:

The lines from N–S and W–E are used to help draw the church in exactly the right place.

Exercise E

Draw a box the same size as this sketch, and mark on the lines N–S, and W–E.

Exercise F

1. Draw the church on to your sketch.
2. Copy the sketch of the car park in the right place on your sketch.

Exercise G

Put these drawings in the right place on your sketch, using the photograph to help you.

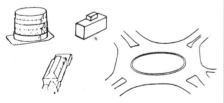

Exercise H

Choose three more buildings from the photograph and copy them on to your sketch.

Exercise I

Explain how the sketch of a street near your school is different from the sketch on this page.

Photograph 2 Doncaster from the air

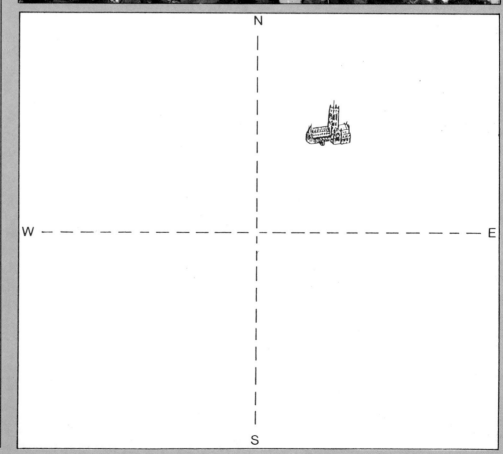

Sketches 3

land use   area
beach   promenade
courts

This section looks at a different type of sketch.

Look at this aerial photograph of part of a city. The photograph shows how the land is used. There are eight different areas. These eight areas are also shown on a simple sketch on the next page.

Photograph: Swansea from the air

M Exercise A

Look at the photograph. Match the letters with the sentence endings. Like this:

D is the sea.

_____ is the sea.
_____ is the beach.
_____ is the rugby ground.
_____ is the car park and promenade.
_____ is the woods.
_____ is a park.
_____ is terraced housing.
_____ is the law courts.

Exercise B

Write five sentences about what you can see in the photograph.

Exercise C

Name two things you can see on this photograph that you will not see on a map of the same place.

Exercise D

Look at the photograph and write five sentences about this city. (Use your answers from Exercise A to help you.)

This type of sketch is called a land use sketch.
The numbers 1–8 show eight areas of this part of the city.

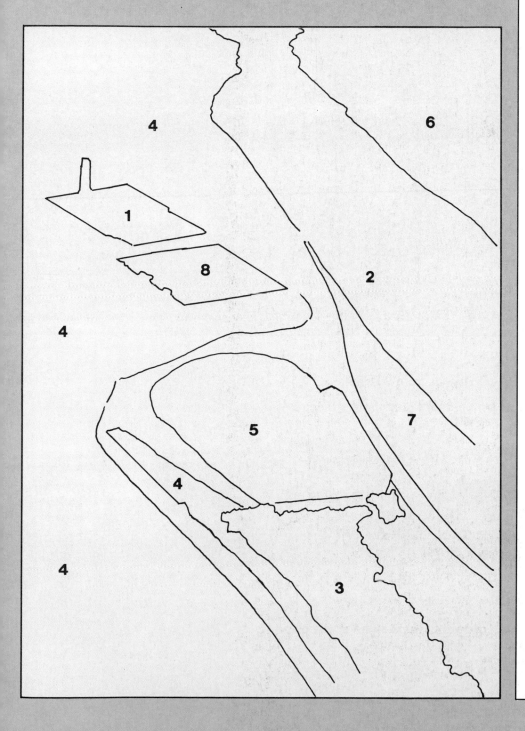

M Exercise E

Look at the land use sketch.
Match the numbers and
sentence endings. Like this:

6 is the sea.

_____	is the sea.
_____	is the beach.
_____	is the rugby ground.
_____	is the car park and promenade.
_____	is the woods.
_____	is a park.
_____	is terraced housing.
_____	is the law courts.

Exercise F

Copy the land use sketch. Then
label it.

Exercise G

Colour your sketch. Use these
colours:
blue for the sea
yellow for the beach
red for the terraced housing
black for the law courts
grey for the car park and
promenade
green for the woods, the park,
and rugby ground

Exercise H

Copy and colour these boxes
under your sketch:

☐ sea
☐ beach
☐ terraced housing
☐ car park and promenade
☐ law courts
☐ woods, park and
   rugby ground

Sketches 4

Key words

centre	buildings
expensive	office
similar	pedestrian
	precinct

This section is about the centre of cities and towns.

The centre of a city is very busy in the daytime. Shops, large stores, banks, cafés and offices are built in city centres. The buildings are often very tall. This saves space.

People go to the city centre to work in the offices, shops and banks. Not many people live there because flats in city centres are very expensive. Most people travel in and out every day by train, car, bus or motorcycle. Young people like to go into the city in the evening. They go to the cinemas, discos, coffee bars and pubs. The bright signs make the city look very different at night.

Photograph: City centre, Leeds

M **Exercise A**

Look at these drawings. Match them with words from this list:

bank / travel agency / large store / cinema / café / pub / hotel / theatre

Answer like this: *1. = cinema*

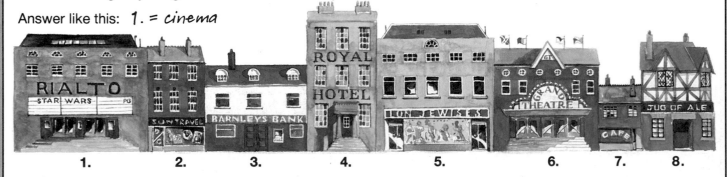

1.   2.   3.   4.   5.   6.   7.   8.

FG **Exercise B**

Write a sentence to explain what each of the buildings in the drawings above is used for:

Begin like this: *1. A cinema is a place where ...*

Important cities have large centres. They have the biggest shops and offices, and there is more to do in the evening. But most city centres and town centres look very similar. The photograph on the opposite page shows the centre of Leeds.

Look at this sketch.
It is a sketch of the city centre in the photograph.

Sketch City centre, Leeds

Exercise C

Copy the sketch of the centre of Leeds.

M **Exercise D**

Match the numbers of the sketch with words from this list:
pedestrian precinct / fur shop / office block / telephone box

Exercise E

Write the words: pedestrian precinct, shop, office block and telephone box on your sketch, in the correct places.

FG **Exercise F**

Copy and complete the sentences below:

A city centre is a very _____ place. The buildings at the _____ are mainly shops and offices. Not many _____ live in city centres, because flats are very _____. Most people who work in the centre _____ in and out every day. At _____, discos, cinemas and coffee bars are _____.

Exercise G

Look at this sketch. It shows a street in a city centre. The names of the shops are missing.
Copy the sketch, but add shop names. Choose the names of some shops from your city centre.

Exercise H

Name five things in your nearest city centre that are not named on these two pages.

Directions 1

Key words

compass   going
pointing   coming
north   south   east   west

This section is about directions.
Left and right and north, south,
east and west are all directions.

Tim must walk left to the door,

He must walk right to the cat.

There are other ways of showing directions. They
can be shown on a plan called a **compass**. This is
a **compass plan**:

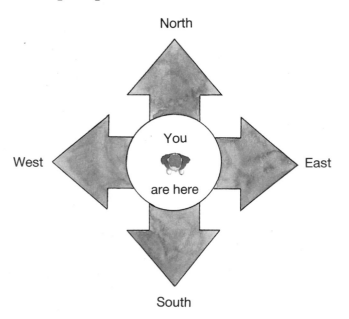

Where Tim is going to

Tim walks this way
He walks in a straight line.
Tim is walking **towards** the east.

East is the direction Tim is going in.

Where Tim is coming from

Now look at where Tim is coming **from**.
Tim is going to the east.
But he is coming **from** the west.
West is the direction Tim is coming from.

Photograph 1

Photograph 2

Look at the drawings on the opposite page and then answer the questions.

CH **Exercise A**

Copy and complete these sentences:

1. The direction Tim walks to get to the door is (left / right).
2. The direction Tim walks to get to the cat is (left / right).

CH **Exercise C**

Look at Photograph 2.

1. The road to Bradford is on the (left / right).
2. The road to Wakefield is on the (left / right).

CH **Exercise B**

Copy and complete these sentences:

1. In Photograph 1 the road to Harrop Fold is to the (left / right / straight on).
2. The road to Bolton by Bowland is (left / right / straight on).
3. The road to Slaidburn is (left / right / straight on).
4. The road to Clitheroe is (left / right / straight on).
5. The road to Grindleton is (left / right / straight on).

Exercise D

Name the direction in which Tim is **going to** in these pictures. Answer like this: *1. East*

1.   2.   3.   4.

Exercise E

Name the direction the line is **pointing to**, and draw the line.

Like this: 1. *East* 2.   3.  4.

Exercise F

Name the direction Tim is **coming from**.

Answer like this: *1. West*

1.   2.   3.   4.

FS **Exercise G**

Do Exercise D again, but this time write where Tim is coming **from**. Like this:

1. Tim is coming from the *west* .
2. Tim is coming from the _____ .
3. Tim is coming from the _____ .
4. Tim is coming from the _____ .

Exercise H

Copy the letters A, B, and C in these boxes:

North   North   North

1. Draw a line going to the south from A.
2. Draw a line going to the west from B.
3. Draw a line going to the east from C.

Directions 2

This section is about more directions on a compass plan.

More lines are needed on the compass plan to show direction. **This compass plan shows eight directions.**

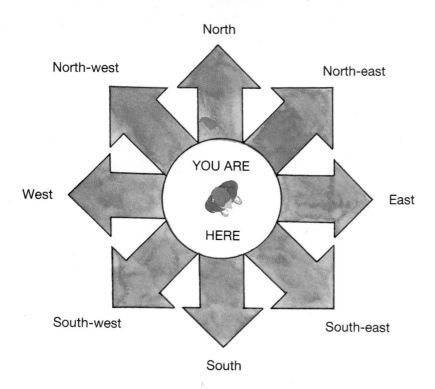

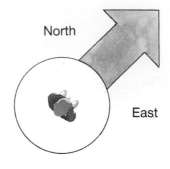

Look at Tim in this picture.
He is not walking towards the north.
He is not walking towards the east.
Tim is walking between north and east.
He is walking towards the **north-east.**

Exercise A

Name the direction Tim is **going to** in these pictures.
Answer like this:
1. *North*

Exercise B

Name the direction Tim is **coming from**.
Answer like this:
1. *South-west*

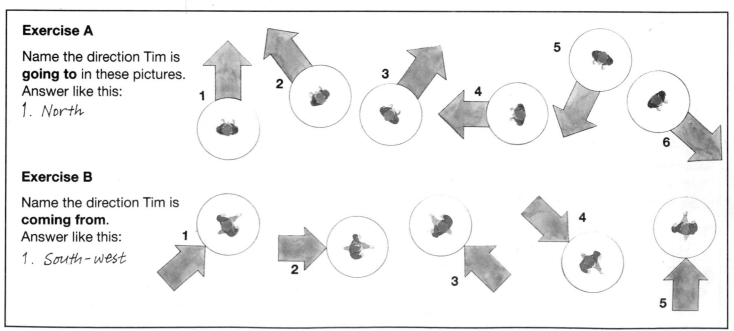

Directions on a compass may be shown by numbers as well as names. The numbers are called **degrees**, and they are shown like this °. So ten degrees is written as 10°.

The needle on the compass always points to the north. South is in a direction of 180° from north, as this photograph shows:

This drawing shows a group of friends sitting at a table. Ashok is sitting on the north side of the table. Lee is sitting on the south side of the table. Like this:

M **Exercise C**

Match the names and the sentence endings.

Ashok / Sita / Dawn / Ben

1. _____ is west of Joanne.
2. _____ is north-east of Fran.
3. _____ is north of Lee.
4. _____ is south-east of Tom.

FS **Exercise D**

Copy and complete the sentences, by naming the directions.

1. The direction from Sita to Joanne is _____.
2. The direction from Dawn to Tom is _____.
3. The direction from Ashok to Lee is _____.
4. The direction from Lee to Ashok is _____.
5. The direction from Fran to Ben is _____.

Exercise E

Copy this compass plan, and write in the missing degrees, like this:

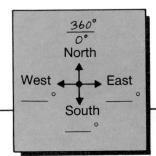

T/F **Exercise F**

Write true or false. Like this: *1. true*

1. From Sita to Joanne, the direction is east.
2. From Ben to Fran, the direction is south-west.
3. From Dawn to Tom, the direction is north-east.
4. From Ashok to Lee, the direction is north.
5. From Tom to Dawn, the direction is south-east.

CH **Exercise G**

Look at the photograph of the compass showing directions in degrees. Copy and complete the sentences below:

1. South is (180° / 240°) from north.
2. East is (20° / 90°) from north.
3. West is (160° / 270°) from north.
4. North-east is (45° / 300°) from north.
5. South-east is (135° / 225°) from north.

Exercise H

Plan a journey around your school and name the directions when you change course on your journey. (Try to have about five changes of direction.)

Directions 3

Key words

roundabout   church
supermarket   building

This section is about directions on a map.

Look at this street plan of a town. In the centre of the town there is a big roundabout.

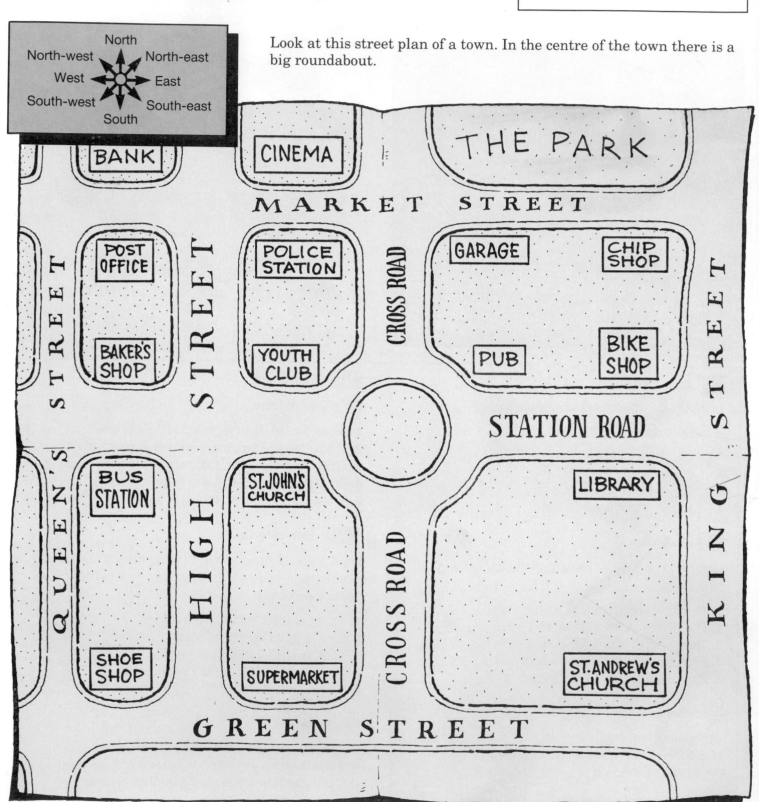

M **Exercise A**

Match the names with the sentence endings:

> High street / King Street
> Market Street / Green Street

1. _____ is north of the roundabout.
2. _____ is south of the roundabout.
3. _____ is east of the roundabout.
4. _____ is west of the roundabout.

M **Exercise B**

Match the names with the sentence endings:

> The bank / The garage /
> St. Andrew's church / The shoe shop

1. _____ is south-east of the bus station.
2. _____ is north-west of the police station.
3. _____ is south-west of the library.
4. _____ is north-east of the youth club.

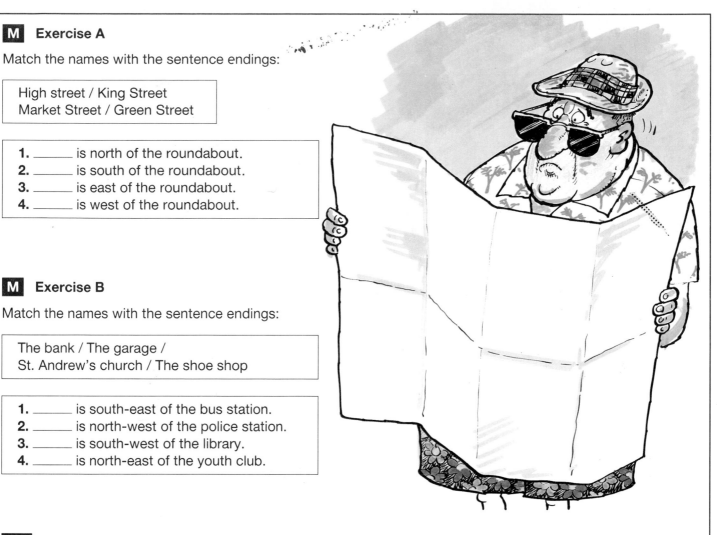

T/F **Exercise C**

Write true or false, for the sentences below. Answer like this: *1. true*

1. The police station is north of the youth club.
2. The bank is west of the cinema.
3. The supermarket is south of St. John's church.
4. The pub is east of the bike shop.
5. The post office is north-west of St. Andrew's church.
6. The supermarket is south-west of the library.
7. The chip shop is north-east of the shoe shop.
8. The cinema is south-east of the library.

Exercise D

1. Name a building in the north-east part of town.
2. Name a building in the south-west part of town.
3. Name a building in the south-east part of town.
4. Name a building in the north-west part of town.

Exercise E

Copy this simple street plan.

1. Draw a bank in the north of town.
2. Draw a church in the south of town.
3. Draw a shop in the west of town.
4. Draw a garage in the east of town.
5. Name the streets on your plan.

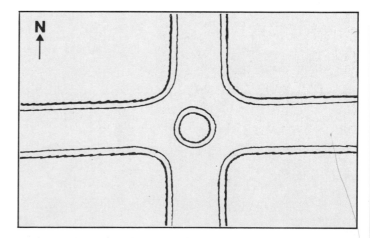

Directions 4

This section is about directions in the British Isles.

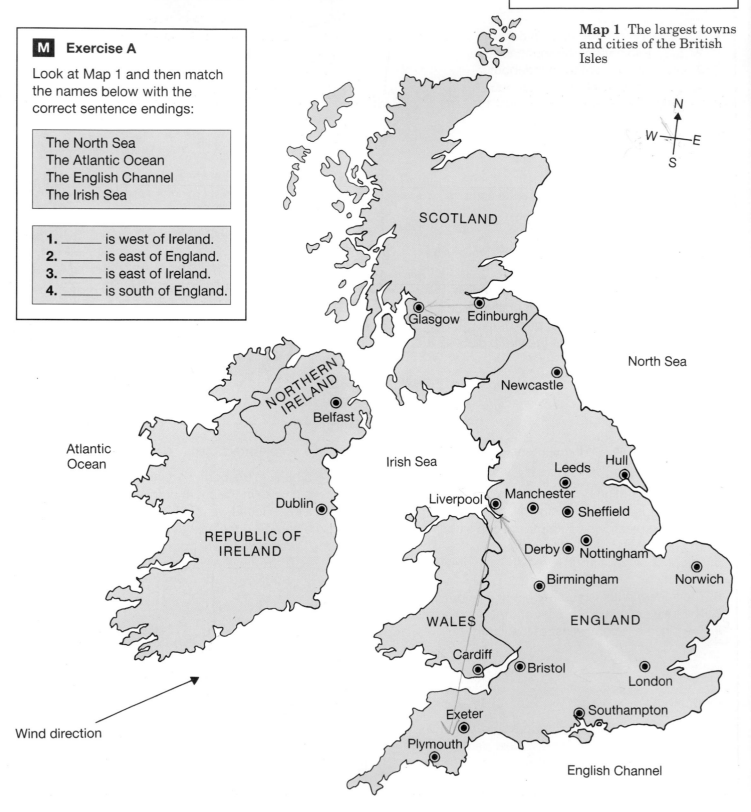

Map 1 The largest towns and cities of the British Isles

M Exercise A

Look at Map 1 and then match the names below with the correct sentence endings:

The North Sea
The Atlantic Ocean
The English Channel
The Irish Sea

1. _____ is west of Ireland.
2. _____ is east of England.
3. _____ is east of Ireland.
4. _____ is south of England.

SCOTLAND

Glasgow Edinburgh

North Sea

Newcastle

NORTHERN IRELAND

Belfast

Atlantic Ocean

Irish Sea

Hull

Leeds

Liverpool Manchester

Sheffield

Dublin

Derby Nottingham

REPUBLIC OF IRELAND

Birmingham

Norwich

WALES

ENGLAND

Cardiff

Bristol

London

Exeter

Southampton

Wind direction

Plymouth

English Channel

CH **Exercise B**

Look at Map 1, and then copy and complete the sentences below. Choose the correct word in the brackets.

1. The country north of England is called (Wales / Scotland / Republic of Ireland)
2. The country east of Wales is called (the Republic of Ireland / England / Scotland).
3. The country north-east of Northern Ireland is called (England / Wales / Scotland).
4. The country west of Wales is called (England / the Republic of Ireland/Scotland).
5. The country north-east of the Republic of Ireland is called (Northern Ireland / Wales / England).
6. The winds which blow across the British Isles come mainly from the (south-west / south-east).

M **Exercise C**

Look at Map 1, and then copy and complete the sentences below.

1. London is (south-east/south-west) of Birmingham.
2. Bristol is (east / west) of London.
3. Newcastle is (north-east / south-east) of Liverpool.
4. Liverpool is (north-west / south-east) of Birmingham.
5. Glasgow is (west / east) of Edinburgh.
6. Plymouth is (south-east / south-west) of Liverpool.
7. Dublin is (west / east) of Liverpool.
8. Norwich is (west / east) of Birmingham.
9. Leeds is (north / south) of Sheffield.
10. Hull is (east / west) of Leeds.

M **Exercise D**

Look at Map 2 and then match the names below with the correct sentence endings:

> Tyne Tees / Ulster TV /
> Granada TV / Grampian /
> TSW / TVS / Anglia

1. _____ is watched in south-west England.

2. _____ is watched in south-east England.

3. _____ is watched in northern Scotland.

4. _____ is watched in north-east England.

5. _____ is watched in eastern England.

6. _____ is watched in Northern Ireland.

7. _____ is watched in north-west England.

Map 2 The United Kingdom's ITV regions

GRAMPIAN

SCOTTISH TV

ULSTER TV

BORDER TV

TYNE TEES

GRANADA

YORKSHIRE TV

HTV

CENTRAL

ANGLIA

TSW

TVS

THAMES LWT

Symbols 1

This section is about using signs. The signs are called symbols.

Look at these signs. You can see them in most towns. Traffic signs are simple. This makes them easy to read.

Figure 1

A.   B.   C.

D.   E.   F.

G.   H.

M Exercise A

Match the letters by the signs with the correct meanings.

No motor vehicles
No right turn
No cycling
No left turn
Slippery road
Roadworks
Roundabout
Hump bridge

M Exercise B

Look at Figure 2. Copy the signs and match them with the words below:
disabled/no smoking/telephone

Exercise C

Make up your own signs for these places at your school.

1. Gymnasium.
2. Science department.
3. Play area.
4. Library.
5. Craft, design, and technology (CDT) area.

Figure 2

This is a windmill:

This is a sketch of the windmill:

This is also a drawing to show a windmill.
This is easy and quick to draw. It does not show everything about the windmill.
It is the **symbol** for a windmill.
A symbol stands for something important.

Sometimes letters can be used as symbols on a map:
   P is the symbol for a post office.
   T is the symbol for a telephone box.
The first letter of the word is used as the symbol.

M **Exercise D**

Here are some symbols. Copy them and write down what you think they mean. Choose your answers from the list below. Write your answers like this: 〤 *is the symbol for a windmill*

windmill / church / bridge / quarry / lighthouse / heliport

1.   2.   3.

4.   5.   6.

M **Exercise E**

Match these symbols with their meanings.

TH / MP / PH / CH

1. _____ means public house.
2. _____ means club house.
3. _____ means mile post.
4. _____ means town hall.

Exercise F

Draw your own map symbols for:

1. Café
2. Petrol station
3. Ice rink
4. Public library

Symbols 2

This section is about the symbols used on a weather map.

These are typical weather maps.

Figure 1

Figure 2

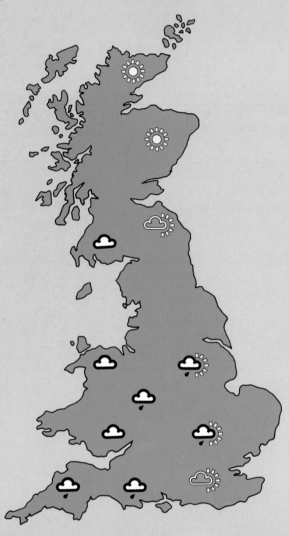

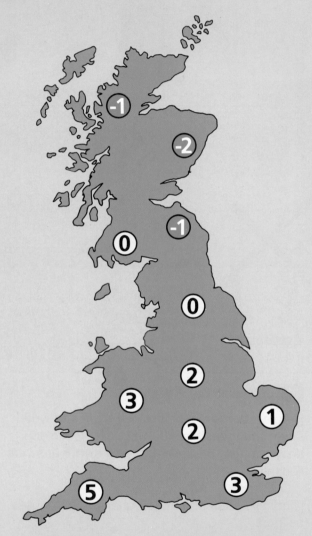

This is what weather map symbols mean:

 is the symbol for rain.

is the symbol for fine weather.

is the symbol for dull weather.

is the symbol for sunny intervals.

Wind speed and direction are shown like this

 is the symbol for rain and sunny intervals.

is the symbol for snow.

 is the symbol for sleet.

 is the symbol for a thunderstorm.

FOG is written on the map in words.

The map can also show how hot or cold it is. This means it can show temperature. Numbers on the map show temperature. Like this:

Temperatures less than 0, like −2, mean it is freezing.
Temperatures between 0 and 5 mean it is cold.
Temperatures between 5 and 10 mean it is cool.
Temperatures between 10 and 15 mean it is mild.
Temperatures between 15 and 20 mean it is warm.
Temperatures between 20 and 25 mean it is hot.
Temperatures above 25 mean it is very hot.

The numbers mean **degrees Celsius**.
So five degrees Celsius is written 5°C, for short, and 5 on the map.

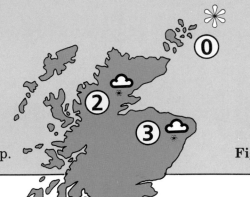

Figure 3

Exercise A

Draw the cloud symbol for the weather today.

FS **Exercise B**

Look at Figure 1 on the opposite page and finish the sentences below.

1. The weather in north Wales is _____ .
2. The weather in south-east England is _____ .
3. The weather in north-east Scotland is _____ .
4. The weather in south-west England is _____ .

FS **Exercise C**

Look at Figure 2 on the opposite page, and finish the sentences below:

1. The temperature in central Wales is _____ .
2. The temperature in central England is _____ .
3. The temperature in eastern England is _____ .
4. The temperature in north-west Scotland is _____ .

Exercise D

What do the temperatures below mean?
Answer like this:

1. 3°C means it is cold.

1. 3°C **2.** 8°C **3.** 22°C **4.** 16°C **5.** 11°C
6. −2°C **7.** 6°C **8.** −3°C **9.** 26°C **10.** 0°C

Exercise E

Look at Figure 3. Choose any five parts of the country and write a sentence for each one to describe the weather. Like this:

The weather in South-east England is rainy, and the temperature is 8°C.

Exercise F

Keep a record of the weather for a week by using the symbols. Draw a chart like this:

Monday	Tuesday	Wednesday	Thursday	Friday	Saturday	Sunday

Symbols 3

Key words

crops   dairy
wheat   market garden
arable   vegetables

This section is about farming in Britain.

The weather is very important to a farmer. Different plants grow in different types of weather. Plants grown on a farm are called **crops**. Crops like potatoes and wheat, are grown as food for people. Other crops may be grown to feed animals. These are called fodder crops.

This photograph shows an **arable farm**. An arable farmer grows food crops, like vegetables and cereals. Wheat, barley and oats are cereal crops. East Anglia is a good place for arable farming. Here are some things grown on an arable farm:

Photograph 1   Arable farm

This photograph shows a **dairy farm**. Dairy cows give milk. Milk is an important food. Here are some things made from milk:

Devon and Cornwall are good places for dairy farming.

Some places have dairy farms and grow crops as well. This is called **mixed farming**.

A **market garden** grows vegetables, flowers and fruit. Sometimes greenhouses are used on a market garden. Growing plants and vegetables under glass keeps them warm.

Here are some things grown on a market garden:

Photograph 2   Dairy farm

A **hill farmer** looks after sheep and some beef cattle. Sheep farms are found in the hills and mountains. The weather is too cold and wet to grow a lot of crops. The land is too steep, and the soil is too thin and stony for crops. The sheep are tough. They have to live through very cold winters. Roads to sheep farms in winter may be blocked by snow.

Photograph 3 Hill farm

M Exercise A

Match the words with the symbols:

Words

Dairy farming / Arable farming / Hill farming / Market gardening / Mixed farming

Symbols

A   B   C   D   E

M Exercise B

Match the weather symbols with the right type of farming:

Types of farming

Market gardening / Hill farming / Dairy farming

Symbols

FG Exercise C

Look at the photographs of the types of farming. Use the symbols below to complete the sentences. Like this:

1. Hill farmers get lots of snow in winter.

1. Hill farmers get lots of ❄ in winter.
2. Arable farmers use 🚜 in their fields.
3. Dairy farmers have lots of 🐄 .
4. Sheep farms are in the ⛰ and hills.
5. Milk is taken away by a 🚚 .

Exercise D

Look at the drawings on the opposite page.

1. Name the things made from milk.
2. Name the things grown on a market garden.
3. Draw your own symbols to show things grown on an arable farm.

CH Exercise E

Look at the map and complete the sentences:

1. Western Britain is more important for (hill / dairy) farming.
2. Eastern Britain is more important for (hill / dairy) farming.
3. Cornwall is important for (arable / dairy) farming.
4. East Anglia is important for (arable / hill) farming.
5. Wales is important for (market / hill) farming.

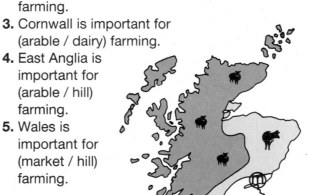

Map Britain showing types of farming

Hill farming
Dairy farming
Arable farming
Market gardening

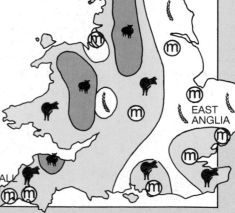

CORNWALL

EAST ANGLIA

Symbols 4

This section is about using colour as a symbol. It is also about the weather of the British Isles.

The weather is not always the same everywhere in the British Isles. The weather is also different at different times of the year. In winter it is cold. In summer it is usually warm. Some parts of the British Isles are colder than others, in winter. Some parts of the British Isles are warmer than others, in summer.

Look at the map below. It shows temperatures in summer. It uses colour as a map symbol.

This colour [ ] shows the warmest places.

This colour [ ] shows warm places.

This colour [ ] shows cool places.

The coloured boxes are called a key. They are called a key because they 'unlock' the map. A map without a key does not show us anything.

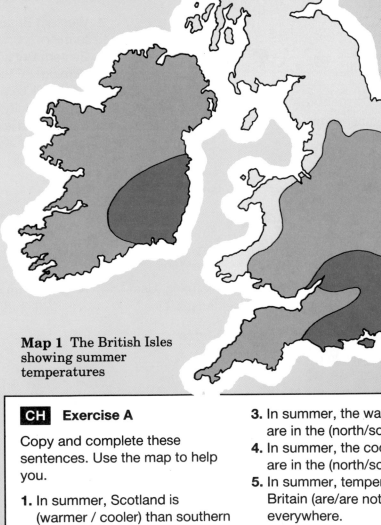

■ Warmest places
■ Warm places
□ Cool places

Map 1 The British Isles showing summer temperatures

CH   **Exercise A**

Copy and complete these sentences. Use the map to help you.

1. In summer, Scotland is (warmer / cooler) than southern England.
2. In summer, the north is (warmer / cooler) than the south.
3. In summer, the warmest places are in the (north/south).
4. In summer, the coolest places are in the (north/south).
5. In summer, temperatures in Britain (are/are not) the same everywhere.

Look at this map. It shows the temperature of the British Isles in winter.

T/F Exercise B

Look at the map showing temperatures in winter. Copy the sentences, and then write true or false.

1. The south-west is mild in winter.
2. The coldest parts of Britain in winter are in the east.
3. The temperatures in winter are the same everywhere.
4. Temperatures decrease from west to east.
5. The north of Scotland is colder than the Isle of Wight.
6. In winter it is mild in the west, but cold in the east.

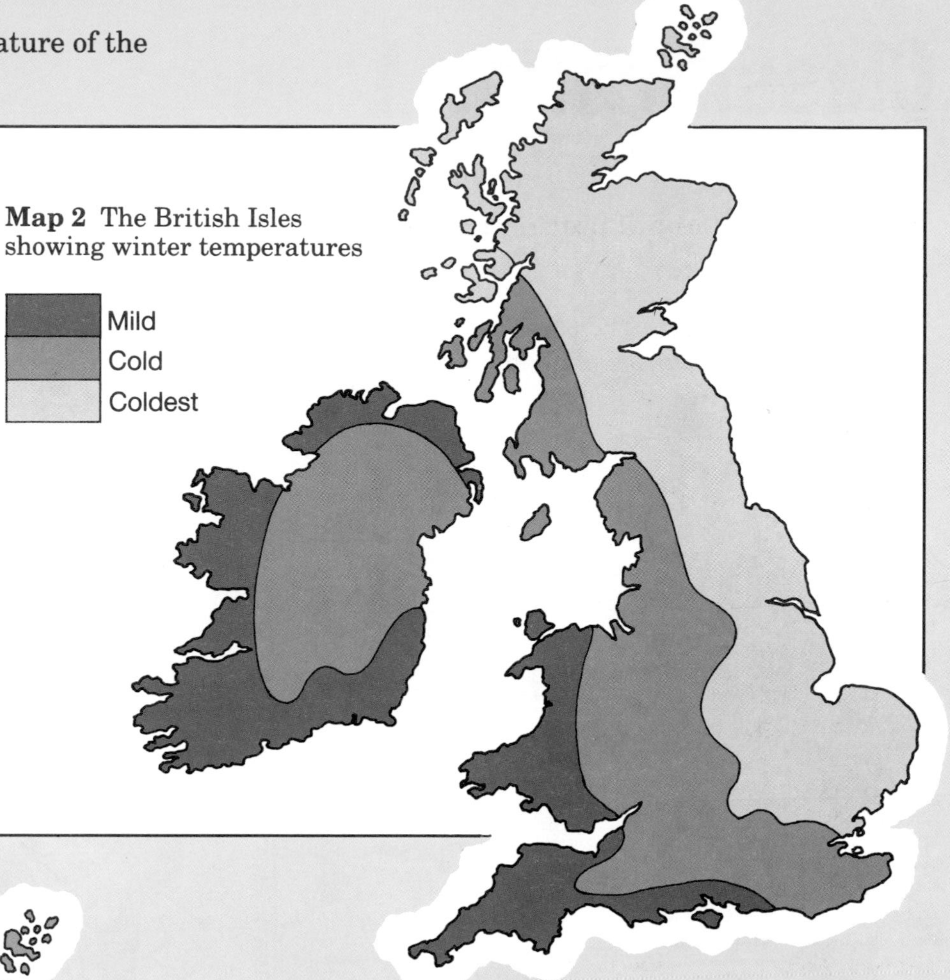

Map 2 The British Isles showing winter temperatures

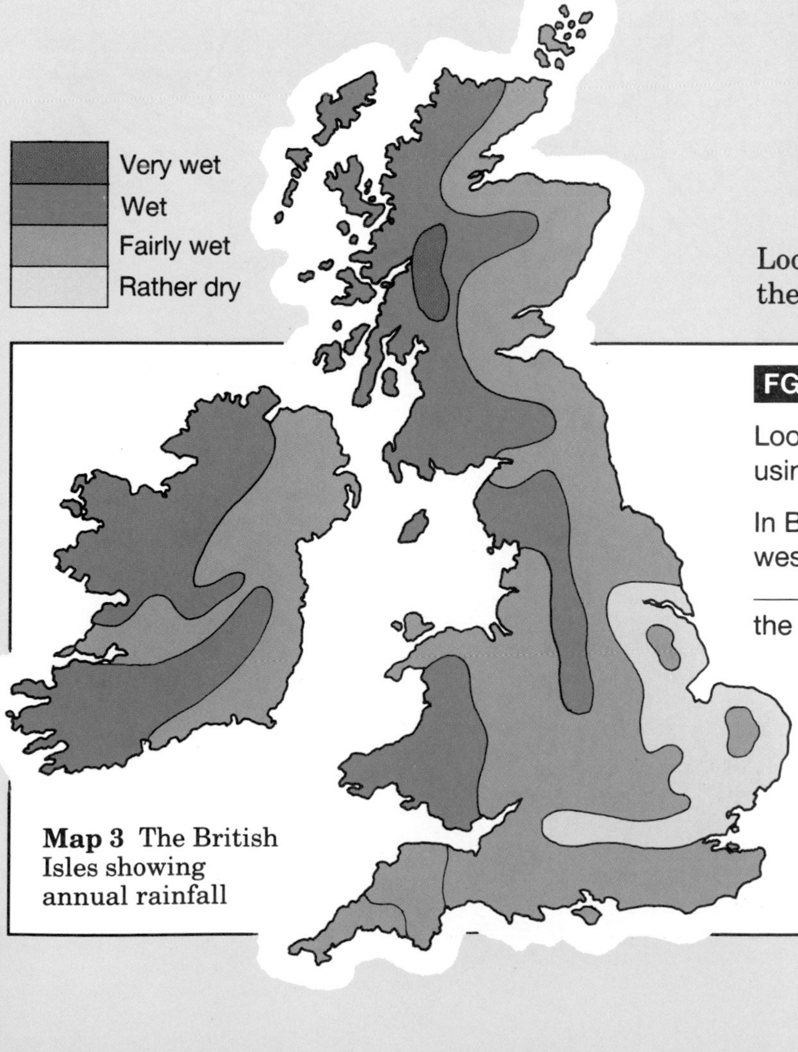

- Mild
- Cold
- Coldest

- Very wet
- Wet
- Fairly wet
- Rather dry

Map 3 The British Isles showing annual rainfall

Look at this map. It shows how much rain falls in the British Isles every year.

FG Exercise C

Look at the rainfall map. Complete the sentences, using words from the list below:

In Britain, some parts are _____ than others. The western parts of _____ are wetter than the eastern _____. The winds passing over Britain _____ from the west. This means that _____ Britain gets the rain first. These _____ are drier when they reach _____ Britain. So eastern Britain gets _____ rain.

western / come / less / eastern / wetter / Britain / parts / winds

Classification 1

Key words

groups
classification

This section is about putting things into groups. This is called classification.

Look at these drawings of people at work:

1. A builder

2. A farm worker

3. A waiter

4. A teacher

5. A computer operator

6. A bus driver

7. A doctor

8. A steel maker

Exercise A

Copy the chart. Fill it in. The first line has been done for you.

	Builder	Farm worker	Waiter	Teacher	Computer operator	Bus driver	Doctor	Steel maker
1. People who work indoors			✓	✓	✓		✓	✓
2. People who work outdoors								
3. People who make things								
4. People who serve others								
5. People who use machines								
6. People who have dangerous jobs								
7. People who have clean jobs								
8. People who can work anywhere								

Look at these drawings of buildings:

1. A shop

2. A church

3. A bank

4. A hotel

5. A railway station

6. A football ground

7. A café

8. An airport

Exercise B

Copy the chart. Fill it in. The first one has been done for you.

1. Buildings found in most villages
2. Buildings found in every town
3. Buildings found in every city
4. Buildings found in some parts of the country
5. Buildings that are busy every day
6. Buildings that are busy only on some days

	1 Shop	2 Church	3 Bank	4 Hotel	5 Railway station	6 Football ground	7 Café	8 Airport
	✓	✓						

Exercise C

Bob has filled in the names and addresses of some buildings on a chart.

Copy the chart and fill it in for your home town.

Bob's Home Town

	Name of the building	Address
1. Shop	Brown's, the chemist	Station Road
2. Church	St. Michael's	Wellfield Street
3. Bank	Trusty Bank	Money Road
4. Hotel	The Dragon Hotel	Dunn Terrace
5. Railway station	British Rail	High Street
6. Football ground	Munchester Rovers	Canal Street
7. Café	Joe's Grill	High Street
8. Airport	Heathwick Airport	Heathwick Town

Classification 2

This section is about classifying places in southern England.

Tom lives in a village. He is twelve years old and goes to a secondary school in Brighton. He travels to the town by bus every day.

Look at the map opposite. The schools on the map are all in the county of East Sussex.

A county is made up of villages, towns and cities, and the countryside between. East Sussex is just one county in this part of England. The counties next to East Sussex are called West Sussex, Surrey and Kent.

Map 1 Schools in East Sussex

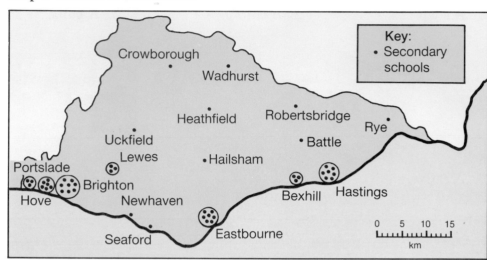

A group of counties is sometimes called a **region**. These counties make up a part of the South-east Region. The map below shows all of the South-east Region.

Map 2 South-east Region of Britain

The Counties

East Sussex
Oxfordshire
Buckinghamshire
Bedfordshire
Hertfordshire
Berkshire
Hampshire
West Sussex
Surrey
Kent

London is the most important city in the British Isles. London is divided into parts called **boroughs**. The boroughs in the centre of London make up Inner London.

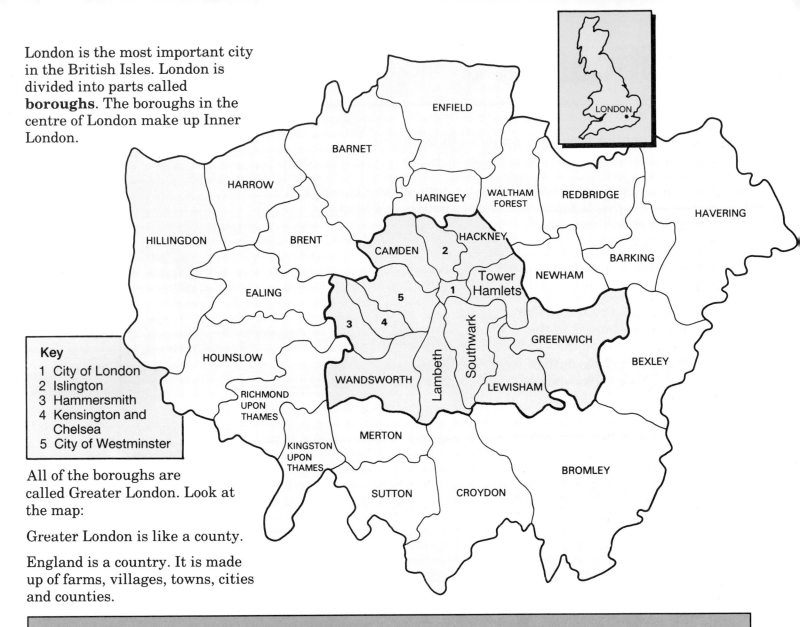

Key
1 City of London
2 Islington
3 Hammersmith
4 Kensington and Chelsea
5 City of Westminster

All of the boroughs are called Greater London. Look at the map:

Greater London is like a county.

England is a country. It is made up of farms, villages, towns, cities and counties.

Exercise A

Look at the map of East Sussex. Copy the headings below. Put the places named on the map under the correct heading. The first one has been done for you:

(a) **Places with 8 schools**
 Brighton

(b) **Places with 7 schools**

(c) **Places with 6 schools**

(d) **Places with 3 schools**

(e) **Places with 1 school**

Exercise B

Look at the map of the South-east Region. Classify this list of towns and cities under the correct heading below:

Abingdon, Aylesbury, Bedford, Brighton, Buckingham, Canterbury, Chichester, Guildford, Hastings, Hertford, Luton, Maidstone, Oxford, Portsmouth, Reading, Reigate, Southampton, Southend, Watford, Windsor, Worthing.
(East Sussex has been done for you)

East Sussex Kent West Sussex Hampshire Berkshire Surrey
Brighton
Hastings

Buckinghamshire Oxfordshire Bedfordshire Hertfordshire

Exercise C

Look at the map of London. Classify the boroughs into groups. You decide how to divide them into groups.

Classification 3

Key words

classifying   region
divided   mountains
separated

SHETLAND ISLANDS

This section is about classifying places in Scotland.

Scotland is a country, but it does not have counties like England and Wales. Scotland is divided into nine regions and three Island Authorities. Look at the map.

There is more than one way to classify a country.

Sometimes the mountains and lowlands divide up a country. The highest part of Scotland is in the north. This part is called the Scottish Highlands. The south of Scotland is high also. This part is called the Southern Uplands. They are separated by a lower part called the Central Lowlands.

All of Scotland's regions can be classified into these three parts. For example, the region called Fife is in the Central Lowlands.

Key

Scottish Highlands

Central Lowlands

Southern Uplands

• Cities

ORKNEY ISLANDS

WESTERN ISLES

HIGHLAND

GRAMPIAN

Elgin

Aberdeen

Map 1 Scotland

TAYSIDE

Perth   Dundee

CENTRAL   FIFE

Glasgow   Edinburgh

LOTHIAN

STRATHCLYDE

BORDERS

DUMFRIES AND GALLOWAY

Exercise A

Look at the map of Scotland

1. Name the regions which have cities.
2. Name the regions in the Scottish Highlands.
3. Name the regions in the Southern Uplands.
4. Name the regions in the Central Lowlands.

Exercise B

Name the regions which have one part in the Scottish Highlands, and one part in the Central Lowlands.

Exercise C

Name the regions which have one part in the Central Lowlands and one part in the Southern Uplands.

Exercise D

Name the three Island Authorities.

Exercise E

Copy and complete the chart below.

Cities	Regions
Glasgow	Strathclyde

The United Kingdom is made up of countries, regions, counties, cities, towns, villages, and farms.

This map shows one way of dividing up the United Kingdom. The map has been divided into 12 parts or regions. It could have been divided into more parts. It could have been divided into fewer parts. See how Scotland has been divided into two regions on this map. On page 56 it is divided into three parts.

There are many ways of classifying a map of the United Kingdom.

When you look at a map, try to divide it into parts. This will make the map clearer to you.

Map 2 Regions of the United Kingdom

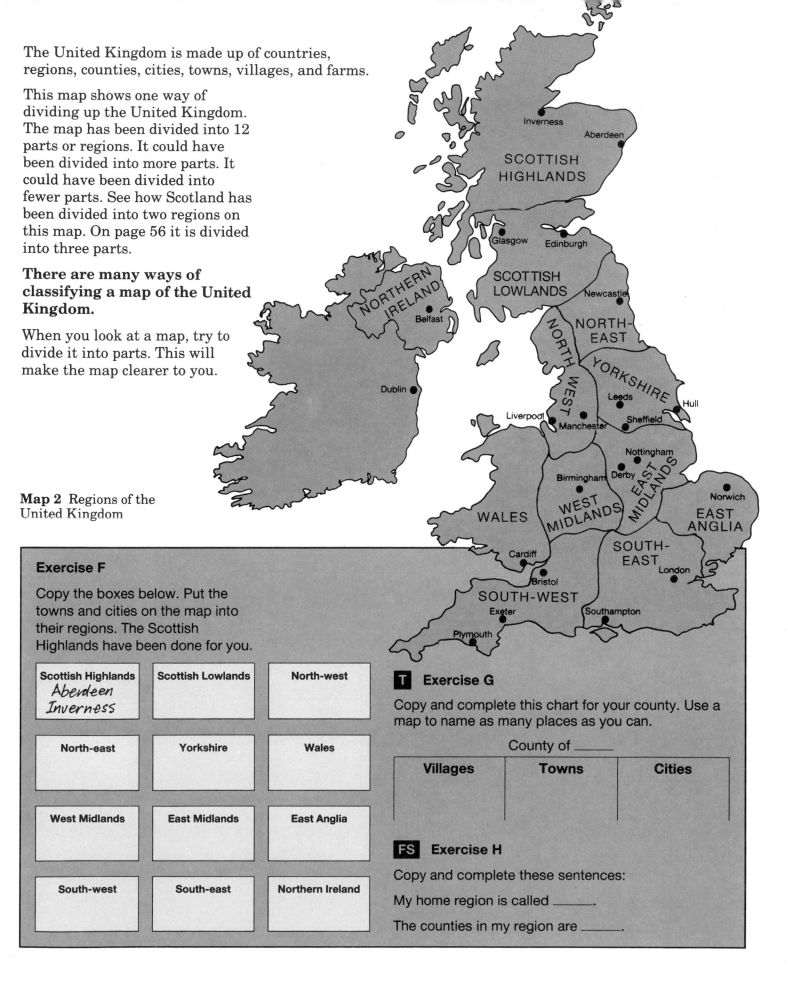

Exercise F

Copy the boxes below. Put the towns and cities on the map into their regions. The Scottish Highlands have been done for you.

Scottish Highlands *Aberdeen* *Inverness*	Scottish Lowlands	North-west
North-east	**Yorkshire**	**Wales**
West Midlands	**East Midlands**	**East Anglia**
South-west	**South-east**	**Northern Ireland**

T Exercise G

Copy and complete this chart for your county. Use a map to name as many places as you can.

County of _____

Villages	Towns	Cities

FS Exercise H

Copy and complete these sentences:

My home region is called _____.

The counties in my region are _____.

Classification 4

Key words

region	population
hills	lowland
mountains	coalfield

This section is about classifying regions in the United Kingdom.

This map is a **population** map. It shows where most people live in the British Isles and where the big towns and cities are.

1. South-west
2. South-east
3. East Anglia
4. East Midlands
5. West Midlands
6. Wales
7. North-west
8. Yorkshire
9. North-east
10. Scottish Lowlands
11. Scottish Highlands
12. Northern Ireland

Map 1
The United Kingdom showing population

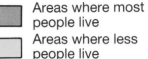

Areas where most people live

Areas where less people live

Areas where few people live

●●● Big towns and cities

Exercise A

Copy the chart. Fill it in.
The first one has been done for you.

1. Regions with more than four big towns

> South-east, West Midlands, North-west, North-east

2. Regions with more than six big towns

3. Regions with more than ten big towns

4. Regions with less than four big towns

5. Regions with areas where few people live

This map shows which regions have hills, mountains, and lowland. The highest mountains are shown by the symbol ▲

Map 2 Highlands and lowlands of the United Kingdom

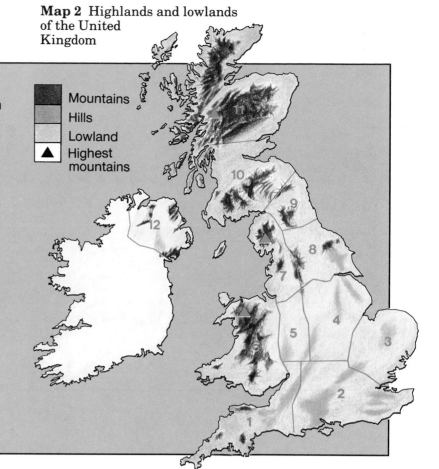

■	Mountains
▦	Hills
☐	Lowland
▲	Highest mountains

Exercise B

Copy the chart. Only a part of the first line has been done for you.

1. Regions with the highest mountains ▲

> *Scottish Highlands, W...*

2. Regions with mountain areas

3. Regions with hill areas

4. Regions with no hills or mountains

5. Regions next to the sea

This map shows the regions with the most coal under the ground.

Map 3
Coalfields of the United Kingdom

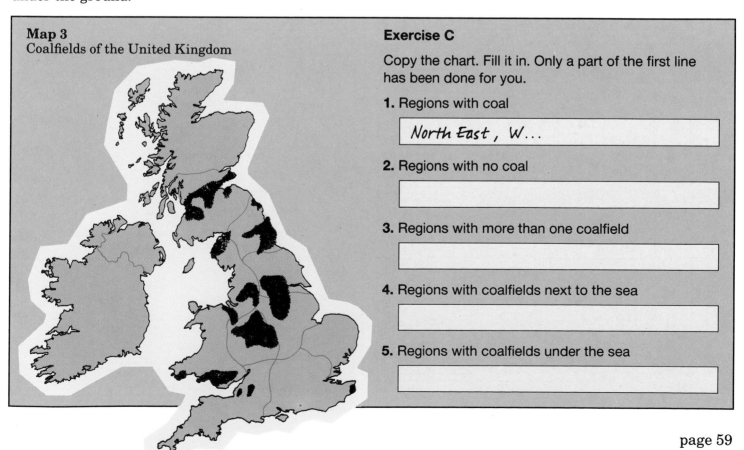

Exercise C

Copy the chart. Fill it in. Only a part of the first line has been done for you.

1. Regions with coal

> *North East, W...*

2. Regions with no coal

3. Regions with more than one coalfield

4. Regions with coalfields next to the sea

5. Regions with coalfields under the sea

Networks 1

Key words

straight   curved
trace   route
journey

This section is about different kinds of lines.

This is a straight line ──────   This is a wavy line ⌒⌒

This is a dotted line – – – – – – .   This is a curved line ⌒

This is a thick line ━━━━━   This is a thin line ──────

M Exercise A

Match the words with the lines. Draw the lines each time.

1. A thick dotted line
2. A dotted curved line
3. A thin wavy line
4. A straight thin line

T Exercise B

Trace the route from A to B in Puzzle 1.
Trace the route from C to D in Puzzle 2.
What do you notice about the shapes you have traced?

Puzzle 1

Puzzle 2

Look at the plan below. It shows the positions of some children in the yard. It shows where they are when the bell goes. The plan also shows how Tom leaves the yard.

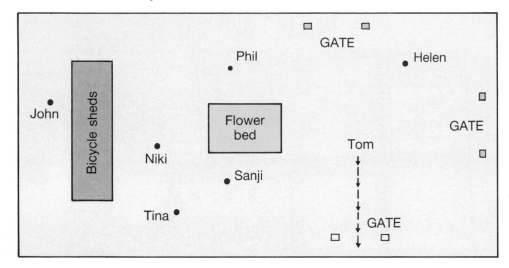

Look at this plan. It shows some shops. Ann has to go to the baker's shop, the chemist, the post office and the supermarket.

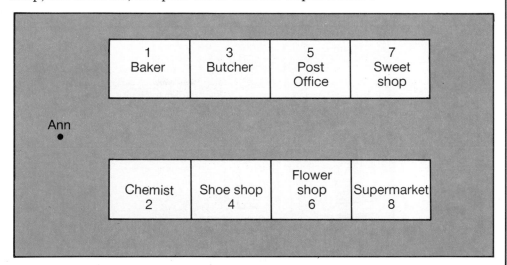

This simple plan shows Ann's journey to the shops. Her journey to the baker, the chemist, the post office and the supermarket is shown by a dotted line:

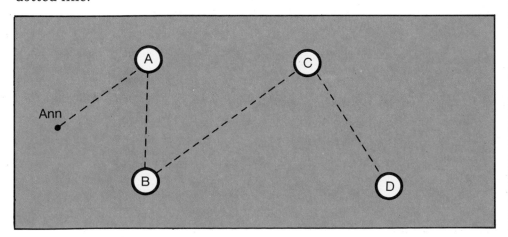

Exercise C

Look at the the plan of the school yard.

1. Copy the plan.
2. Draw the different lines to show how everyone leaves the yard.

Exercise D

Look at Ann's shopping list for today:

> A stamp
> A loaf of bread
> A cabbage
> A packet of sweets

Draw a simple plan to show her journey to the shops.

Exercise E

Write your own shopping list for Ann, and draw lines to show her journey to the shops.

Exercise F

Draw a simple plan to show a journey you make to your shops.

Exercise G

Draw a plan to show which rooms you go to in school today.

Networks 2

This section is about bus journeys.

Wayne lives near the town centre.
Four bus routes go past his house.
Look at the map:

Map 1 Bus routes

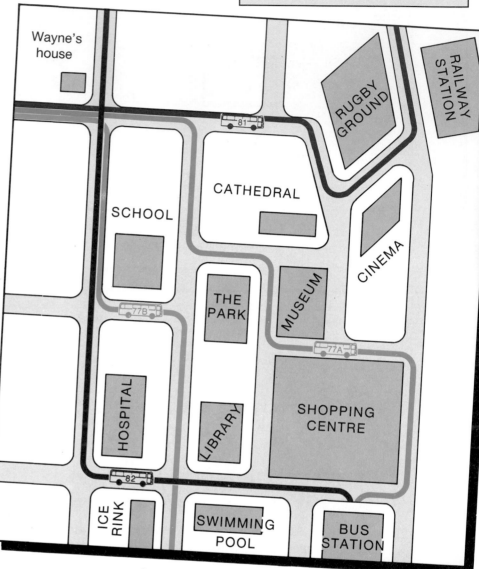

Bus routes: Number 77A   Number 81
            Number 77B   **Number 82**

M **Exercise A**

Match the sentence beginnings with the correct endings.

> Bus number 81 / Bus number 77B
> Bus number 77A / Bus number 82

1. _____ goes past the library.
2. _____ goes past the hospital.
3. _____ goes past the railway station.
4. _____ goes past the museum.

T/F **Exercise B**

Write true or false.

Answer like this: *1. true*

1. Wayne catches the 77B to school.
2. The 82 bus goes past the swimming pool.
3. The 77A goes to the railway station.
4. The 81 goes past the cinema.
5. The 77B goes past the museum.
6. The 82 and 77A go to the shopping centre.

Pat lives in a small village called Trimdon. It is in North-east England. Find it on the map.

Pat likes to go to the towns nearby. There is a leisure centre in Billingham. There is a cinema in Darlington. Pat likes to go shopping in Hartlepool, or sometimes Newcastle and Sunderland. Sometimes she goes to Durham, where there is a cathedral.

Pat goes to town on a bus from Trimdon. The number of each bus route is shown on the map. Pat sometimes has to change buses at the next village. This village is called Sedgefield.

The lines showing the bus routes make a pattern. The pattern of lines is called a **network**.

Map 2 North-east England

Key

Bus route

Newcastle

Sunderland

NORTH SEA

X 2

T 12

Durham

T 11

X 2

Trimdon   T11

T12   Hartlepool

Sedgefield

T12   S 10

S 9   Billingham

S 9   Stockton   S10   Middlesbrough

Darlington

Exercise C

In each question, name the bus service. Answer like this: *1. T11*

1. The bus from Trimdon to Hartlepool.
2. The bus from Trimdon to Durham.
3. The bus from Trimdon to Sedgefield.
4. The bus from Sedgefield to Darlington.
5. The bus from Sedgefield to Middlesbrough.
6. The bus from Sedgefield to Newcastle.
7. The bus from Trimdon to Sunderland.
8. The bus from Sedgefield to Stockton.

T/F ### Exercise D

Write *true* or *false*.

1. Pat must change buses to go to Newcastle.
2. Pat must change buses to go to Sunderland.
3. Pat must change buses to go to the leisure centre.
4. Pat must change buses to go to the cinema.
5. Pat must change buses to go to Durham Cathedral.

Exercise E

1. Copy this simple map.
2. On the map draw your own bus network.
3. Write three sentences about your network.

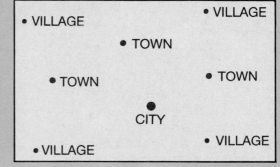

• VILLAGE   • VILLAGE

• TOWN

• TOWN   • TOWN

• CITY

• VILLAGE   • VILLAGE

Networks 3

Key words

junction   motorway
flyover   minor
dual carriageway

This section is about long road journeys in the British Isles.

Photograph 1

Photograph 2

Photograph 3

Sometimes we have to make a special journey, to go on holiday or to visit relatives. Special journeys are longer than the ones we make every day. They take more time and cost more money.

The most important roads in Britain are called **motorways**. Cars, lorries and coaches can travel quickly on motorways. On a special journey, most people will use a motorway at some time. The name of a motorway has the letter **M** and a number like M1, M2 and M56.

Other important roads are called **A** roads, like A30, A65 and A9. Some **A** roads may have two lanes. These roads are called **dual carriageways.**

Roads that are not so important as motorways and **A** roads are called **minor** roads. Some minor roads have names like B127 or B42, but they do not all have names.

The pattern of roads is called a **road network**. The map shows the road network in England, Scotland, and Wales.

Map Road Network

page 65

CH **Exercise A**

Look at the photographs and copy and complete these sentences.

1. Photograph (1 / 2 / 3) is a motorway junction.
2. Photograph (1 / 2 / 3) is a motorway flyover.
3. Photograph (1 / 2 / 3) is a motorway through countryside.

T/F **Exercise B**

Look at the map of the road network. Copy these sentences and then write true, or false. Like this:

1. The M4 joins Cardiff and London. *true*
2. The M8 joins Glasgow and Edinburgh.
3. The M5 joins Exeter and Birmingham.
4. The M62 joins Leeds and Manchester.
5. The M1 joins Leeds and London.

CH **Exercise C**

Copy these sentences. Choose the correct word in brackets:

1. The M1 joins London and (Leeds / Exeter / Cardiff).
2. The M90 joins Perth and (Glasgow / Edinburgh / Dundee).
3. The M11 joins London and (Leeds / Cambridge / Oxford).
4. The M6 joins Birmingham and (Carlisle / Glasgow / Hull).
5. The M62 joins Manchester and (Birmingham / Leeds / Carlisle).

Exercise D

Choose any two places on the map. Name all the roads needed to make the journey between the two places.

Networks 4

Key words

railway   passenger
electricity   power

This section is about Britain's railway network.

Some people travel to work on trains. Trains that carry people are called passenger trains. People who travel to work on trains are called commuters.

Some trains do not carry people. They move things like coal and steel. They are called goods trains or freight trains.

Today, trains get their power from electricity or oil. A train that uses oil is called a diesel train.

This is the British Rail symbol.

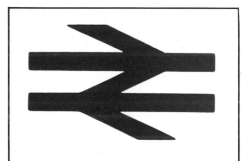

Photograph 1

Photograph 2

M   **Exercise A**

Match the trains with the sentence endings.

> A diesel train / A passenger train / An electric train / A goods train

1. _____ is a train that carries people.
2. _____ is a train that does not carry people.
3. _____ is a train that uses oil.
4. _____ is a train that uses electricity.

Exercise B

Look at the map showing the Inter-City Network, on the next page. Put these stations in the right order, on a journey from London:

Euston / Stoke-on-Trent / Stafford / Manchester / Watford / Rugby / Nuneaton / Milton Keynes

Sometimes on a long journey you have to change trains at different railway stations. Railway journeys to London are shown below. The map is called the Inter-City rail network. On these journeys you do not have to change trains to get to London. The fastest journey times from London are shown on the network.

Exercise C

Write down the times from London. Like this:

1. 1hr. 35min.

1. To Doncaster
2. To Blackpool
3. To Ipswich
4. To Bradford
5. To Manchester
6. To Inverness
7. To Cardiff
8. To Wolverhampton
9. To Hull
10. To your nearest Inter-City station.

Exercise D

In the list below, name the missing stations on a journey to London. Like this: *1. Slough*

1. Swindon, Reading, Paddington
2. Bournemouth, Southampton, Waterloo
3. Norwich, Colchester, Liverpool Street
4. Stafford, Nuneaton, Rugby, Watford, Euston
5. Nottingham, Leicester, Luton, St Pancras
6. Newark, Grantham, Stevenage, King's Cross
7. Birmingham, Coventry, Reading, Paddington
8. Newton Abbot, Exeter, Reading, Slough, Paddington
9. Chesterfield, Derby, Kettering, Luton, St Pancras
10. Worcester, Oxford, Slough, Paddington

Map: Inter-City rail network

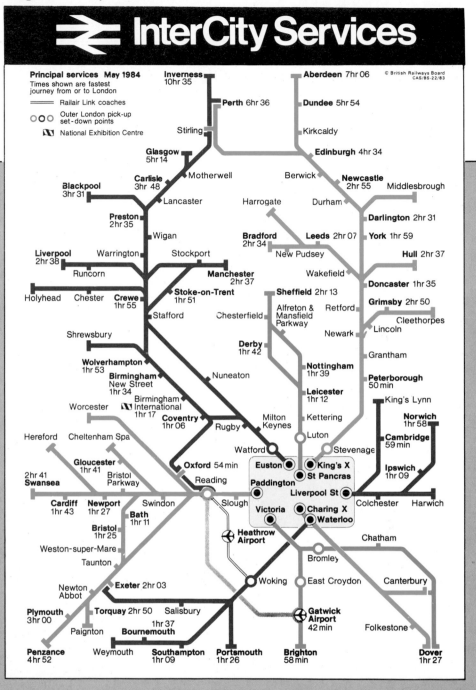

FG Exercise E

Copy and complete the sentences below. Use the map to help you. Like this:

1. Trains from Penzance arrive in London at *Paddington* station.
2. Trains from Liverpool arrive in London at _____ station.
3. Trains from Norwich arrive in London at _____ station.
4. Trains from Derby arrive in London at _____ station.
5. Trains from Lincoln arrive in London at _____ station.
6. Trains from Glasgow arrive in London at _____ station.

Measuring 1

This section is about measuring things.

These are some of the words used in measuring:

length   width   height

Length is the distance from end to end.
Width is the distance from side to side.
Height is the distance from top to bottom.

A ruler helps us to measure things:

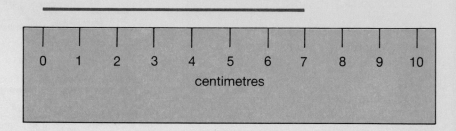

Every mark on the ruler has a number.
The distance between the marks on the ruler is the same every time.
The distance is called a **centimetre**.
The ruler shows length up to 10 centimetres.
The line above the ruler is 7 centimetres long.

One centimetre is worth this much ———
One centimetre is written 1 cm for short.

A centimetre is made from smaller
distances.
The smaller distances are called
millimetres.
One millimetre is worth this much -
Ten millimetres are worth one
centimetre.
One millimetre is written 1 mm, for short.
The line AB is 7 cm 4 mm long.

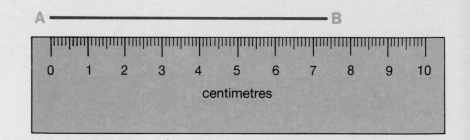

Exercise A

Measure the length of these lines in centimetres. Draw the lines. Answer like this:

Line A is 4 cm long.

A _____

B _____

C _____

D _____

E _____

Exercise B

Measure these lines in centimetres and millimetres. Draw the lines. Answer like this:

Line A is 4 cm 5 mm long.

A _____

B _____

C _____

D _____

E _____

Width

Look at this rectangle. The rectangle is 7 cm long. It is 2 cm wide. Its width is 2 cm. Measure it yourself.

Shape A

Height

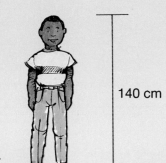

140 cm

This is Linton.
He is really 140 cm tall.
His height is 140 cm.

This is Shirley.
Her height is really 120 cm.
She is not as tall as Linton.
She is 20 cm shorter than Linton.

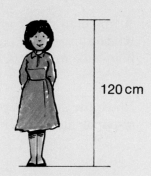

120 cm

Irregular distances

Look at this line. It is 3 cm from A to B. It is 2 cm from B to C. Measure it yourself.

The distance from A to C is 3 cm + 2 cm.

The line from A to C is 5 cm long.

The line from A to C is called an irregular line.

The distance from A to C is called an irregular distance.

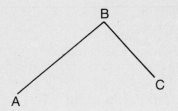

Exercise C

Measure the length and width of these shapes.
Answer like this: *Shape A is 7cm long, 2cm wide.*

Shape B

Shape C

Shape D

Shape E

Exercise D

Measure these irregular distances:

A

B

C

Exercise E

Measure your height and the height of a friend.

Measuring 2

This section is about measuring distances on a map.

A line on a map can be measured without a ruler. Look at the line below, from A to B.

Place the straight edge of a strip of paper along the line. Like this:

Now mark A and B on to the strip of paper. Like this:

Now place the strip of paper along a measuring line. Like this:

It is 8 cm from A to B on the strip of paper. This means the line AB is 8 cm long.

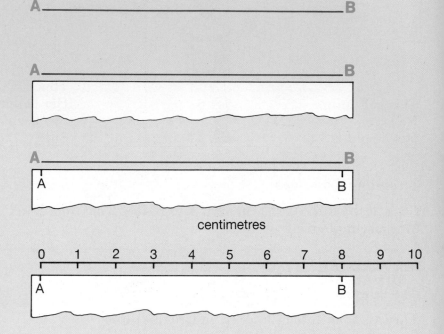

centimetres

0 1 2 3 4 5 6 7 8 9 10

Use this measuring line for Exercise A and Exercise B.

centimetres

1 2 3 4 5 6 7 8 9 10 11 12 13 14 15

millimetres

Exercise A

Use a strip of paper to measure these lines:
Answer like this: *1. 5cm*

1. _____
2. _____
3. _____
4. _____
5. _____
6. _____
7. _____
8. _____

Exercise B

Measure the distances between the dots.
Answer like this: *1. AB = 3cm*

1. A •   • B
2. C•   • D
3.   E •   • F
4. G•   • H
5. J•   • K

On a map, the measuring line shows the real distances between places. These real distances are measured in kilometres or miles. Many signposts show real distances in miles, but sometimes we must write real distances in kilometres.

Look at the map below. It is a map of the south-west of England. The measuring line on the map shows miles. Use the measuring line on the map to answer the exercises below.

Map: South-west England

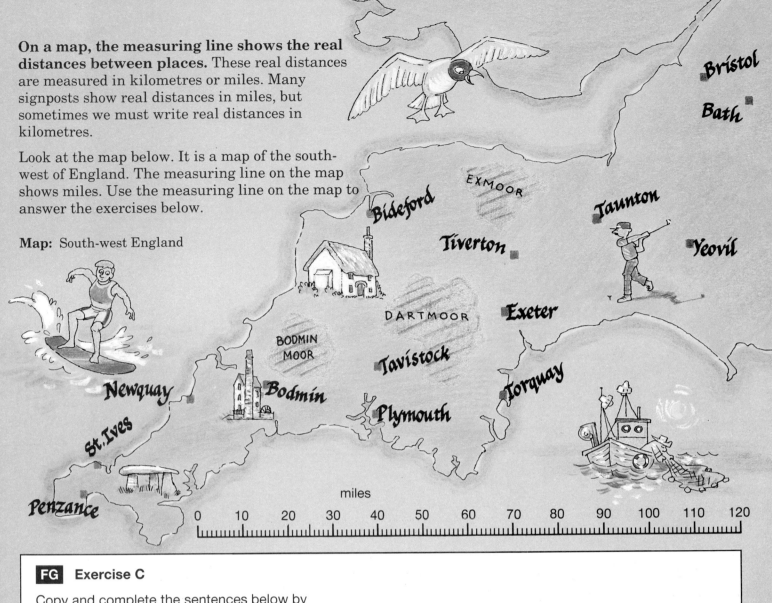

miles
0 10 20 30 40 50 60 70 80 90 100 110 120

FG **Exercise C**

Copy and complete the sentences below by measuring the distances from the map.

1. It is __39__ miles from Yeovil to Tiverton.
2. It is _____ miles from Bristol to Bath.
3. It is _____ miles from Plymouth to Torquay.
4. It is _____ miles from Newquay to Penzance.
5. It is _____ miles from Bristol to Exeter.
6. It is _____ miles from Bideford to Bodmin.

Exercise D

Look at this measuring line showing real distances in kilometres. Use this measuring line to do Exercise C again, but this time write your answers in kilometres like this:

1. It is _____ **kilometres** from Yeovil to Tiverton.

km
0 20 40 60 80 100 120 140 160 180 200

M **Exercise E**

Match the beginnings and the endings of these sentences.

1. Plymouth to Exeter	_____ is 80 miles
2. Bristol to Bideford	_____ is 36 miles
3. Penzance to St. Ives	_____ is 70 miles
4. Exeter to Bath	_____ is 7 miles

Exercise F

Choose one place on the map. Measure how far it is to three other places on the map.

Measuring 3

This section is about problems of measuring in a straight line, on a map.

Problem 1

The measuring line may be too short.

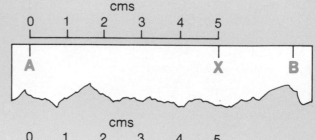

The distance from A to B is more than the measuring line. It is 5 cm from A to X.

The strip of paper can be moved along, like this. We can now see that it is 2 cm from X to B.

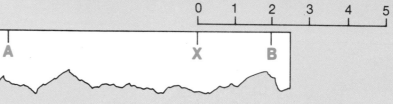

The length of AB is 5 cm + 2 cm. It is 7 cm from A to B.

Problem 2

The measuring line may show only some numbers. Look at this measuring line:

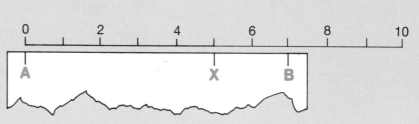

The distance from A to B is more than 6 cm. It is less than 8 cm. It is about 7 cm from A to B. We have to **estimate** the distance AB.

Look at this measuring line:

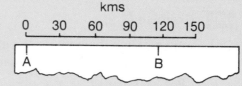

The distance from A to B this time comes from a map. A and B are towns on the map. They are really more than 90 km apart. They are less than 120 km apart. A and B are really about 115 km apart.

Exercise A

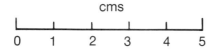

Use this measuring line and a strip of paper, and measure the lines below.

Like this: *A is 4 cm long.*

A _____
B _____
C _____
D _____
E _____
F _____
G _____

Exercise B

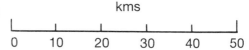

Use this measuring line to find the real distances between the towns below. Answer like this:

1. The real distance between A and B is about 25 km

1. A •   • B

2. C •   • D

3. E •   • F

4. G •   • H

5. J •   • K

This map has a short measuring line, and shows only some numbers:

Map: Towns and cities in England

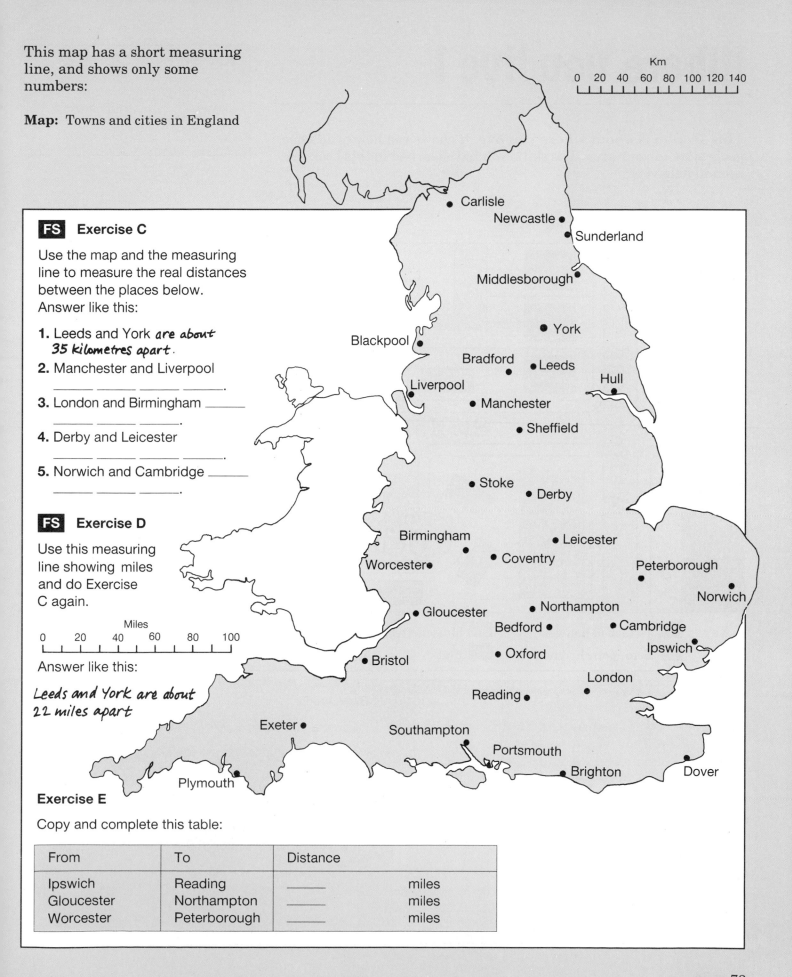

FS **Exercise C**

Use the map and the measuring line to measure the real distances between the places below. Answer like this:

1. Leeds and York *are about 35 kilometres apart*.
2. Manchester and Liverpool
   ___ ___ ___ ___ .
3. London and Birmingham ___
   ___ ___ ___ .
4. Derby and Leicester
   ___ ___ ___ ___ .
5. Norwich and Cambridge ___
   ___ ___ ___ .

FS **Exercise D**

Use this measuring line showing miles and do Exercise C again.

Leeds and York are about 22 miles apart

Exercise E

Copy and complete this table:

From	To	Distance	
Ipswich	Reading	_____	miles
Gloucester	Northampton	_____	miles
Worcester	Peterborough	_____	miles

Where you live 1

This section is about where you live. It shows you how to do some geography in your area. The skills you have learned in this book are used to help you.

—N—

Look at this map of a housing estate.

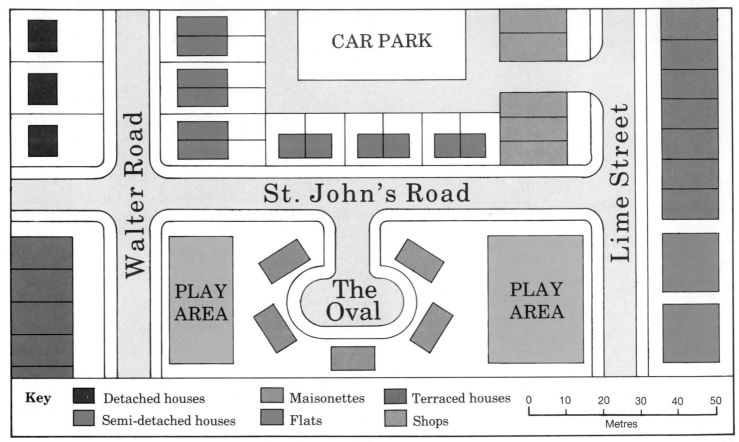

Key ■ Detached houses   ■ Maisonettes   ■ Terraced houses   0 10 20 30 40 50
■ Semi-detached houses   ■ Flats   ■ Shops   Metres

Exercise A

Copy and complete this chart. It classifies the houses on the map. The first line has been done for you.

Types of houses	Number
Detached houses	3
Semi-detached houses	
Terraced houses	
Blocks of flats	
Blocks of maisonettes	
Shops	
Total number of buildings =	

Exercise B

There are ten maisonettes in every block on the map.

How many maisonettes are there altogether on the map?

Exercise C

Describe what you might see on a walk from the terraced houses in Walter Road to the flats in Lime Street.

Exercise D

Look at the photograph of the maisonettes. Make a sketch of them.

M **Exercise E**

These road signs are all on the housing estate. Match the signs with their meanings. Do not draw the signs. Answer like this: A . Crossroads .

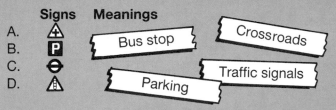

Signs   Meanings

A.
B.
C.
D.

Bus stop
Crossroads
Traffic signals
Parking

Photograph Maisonettes

Exercise F

1. Measure the length of Lime Street, (use the scale line to help you).
2. Measure the length of Walter Road.
3. Measure the length of the terraced houses in Lime Street.

Exercise G

The questions below are about where you live. Len has written his answers for Exercise G. Use them to help you.

Answer these questions:

1. What is the name of your street?
2. What type of house do you live in?
3. Name two people who also live in your street.
4. Do you live on a farm, in a village, in a town or in a city?
5. What is your farm / village / town / city called?

Len's answers

1. Station Road
2. A flat
3. Mrs. Singh and Mr. Thomas
4. A town
5. Newtown

Explore your district

Exercise H

Choose any three streets near your home. Classify the houses in the streets, using the same chart as in Exercise A on page 74.

Exercise J

Copy as many of the signs as you can find, in the streets you have chosen.

Exercise L

Draw your own plan of the streets you have chosen. Mark on your plan the things you think are important.

Exercise I

Draw a sketch of one building in one of the streets you have chosen.

Exercise K

Count the number of steps it takes you to walk the length of your three streets (**be careful!**). Set out your answer like this:

Number of steps

Street 1 (name)
Street 2 (name)
Street 3 (name)

Where you live 2

This section will help you to find places in your district.

Key words

district
information centre
telephone directory

A **map** is the best thing to help you find your way.

Look at this street map. A man has lost his way in Station Road at A. He is trying to get to the library in Wind Street.

Information signs can help us to find some buildings. The man in Station Road should look for this sign:

Finding places without a map, and without signs is difficult. An information centre can help you. The sign for an information centre is:

Exercise A

Write down some directions for the man in Station Road at A. He is trying to get to the library. Start like this:

1. Go to the end of Station Road.
2. Turn left
3. ... .

Exercise B

From the library in Wind Street, the man wants to go to the post office. Write down some directions, to help the man find the post office, from the library.

Exercise C

Draw your own street plan. Mark on it: a shop, a bank and four other buildings. Explain how to get to the shop, from the bank, on your street plan.

M   Exercise D

Match the signs with their meanings.

Answer like this: A = airport

A.   ✈ Gatwick 2 ›

B.   ♿ Toilets ›

C.   🌲 300 yds ›

D.   300 yds ›

toilets / picnic site / airport / camping site

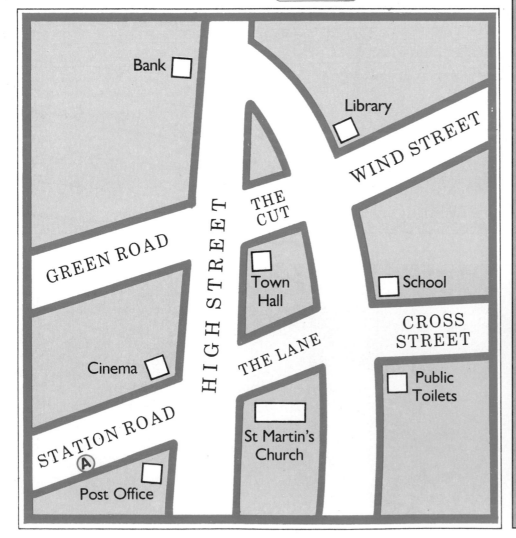

Some buildings are listed in Yellow Pages. This is a telephone directory.

This list shows how some libraries, post offices, pubs and cinemas might look in Yellow Pages.

The map below shows part of a town called Newtown. Look carefully at the map and the Yellow Pages list, before you answer the questions.

Map Newtown

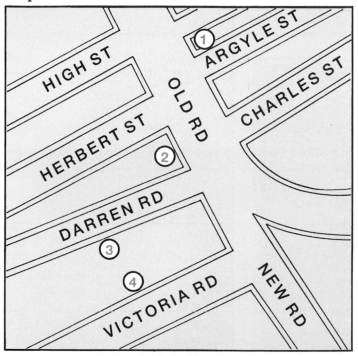

Libraries   Telephone numbers

Atherton, Talbot Rd. .... Atherton 245
Bilton, Alexandra Rd. .... Bilton 802341
Farnworth, Hamilton Terrace .... Farnworth 3317
Newtown, Argyle St. .... Newtown 30156
Sinford, Crescent Road .... Sinford 221333

Cinemas

Globe Theatre, Market St. .... Munchester 221753
Odeon Film Centre, Worcester Pl. .... Sinford 476621
Plaza Cinema, Victoria Rd. .... Newtown 40657
Studio Cinema, West St. .... Burry 774773

Post Offices

Bilton Post Office, Bridge St. .... Bilton 847321
Lergo Post Office, Princess Way .... Lergo 413562
Munchester Post Office, King St. .... Munchester 223311
Newtown Post Office, Darren Rd. .... Newtown 40877

Public Houses

Blue Bell Inn, New Rd. .... Cheddle 4322
Blue Boar Inn, Old Rd. .... Newtown 43755
Boars Head Inn, Henry St. .... Salem 417752
Bridge Inn, Bridge St. .... Sinford 377216

Exercise F

Copy and complete this chart for Newtown:

Building	Telephone number
Library	Newtown 30156
Cinema	
Post Office	
Public House	

Exercise I

Copy and complete this chart for your own home district:

	Address
Your nearest shop	
Your nearest library	
Your nearest school	
Your nearest phone box	
Your nearest post box	
Your nearest bus stop	

Exercise G

Name the streets in Newtown where you would find the library, cinema, post office, and pub. Answer like this: *Library = Argyle Street.*

Exercise H

Match the numbers 1–4 on the map with the words library, cinema, post office and pub.

Exercise J

Copy and complete this chart for your town centre:

	Name and address
The busiest street	
The biggest shop	
The biggest park	
Your favourite place	

Where you live 3

Key words

busiest   region
chart   vehicle
highway code

This section looks at links between your home and other places.

Most places have their busiest spots. It may be a big roundabout on the edge of town. It may be an important crossroads. Look at this road sign:

Type of vehicle	A638 (Bradford)	M606 (Bradford)	M62 (Leeds)	A58 (Leeds)	A638 (Dewsbury)	M62 (Huddersfield)
Cars	139	285	316	124	128	302
Lorries	73	176	215	82	60	175
Coaches	26	62	104	35	30	112
Public buses	13	0	2	14	15	2
Motor bicycles	26	8	15	23	36	25
Vans	44	135	156	56	40	160
Others	35	96	84	46	32	76
			Number of vehicles			

It shows a busy roundabout. The chart above shows the types of vehicles to use the road during a part of the day.

Exercise A

Look at the photograph and name the places where these roads go. Answer like this:

1. Bradford and Dewsbury

1. A638   **3.** M606   **5.** A641
2. M62   **4.** A58

Exercise B

Look at the chart, and find out how many vehicles used each road. Answer like this:

1. A638 Bradford = *356* vehicles.
2. M606 Bradford = ___ vehicles.
3. M62 Leeds = ___ vehicles.
4. M58 Leeds = ___ vehicles.
5. A638 Dewsbury = ___ vehicles.
6. M62 Huddersfield = ___ vehicles.

Exercise C

Look at your answer for Exercise B, and put the roads in order, with the busiest one first.

Exercise D

Copy this simple plan of the roads used in the study:

Colour the roads on your plan like this:

Red   = busiest road.
Blue   = 2nd busiest road.
Green = 3rd busiest road.
Yellow = 4th busiest road.
Brown = 5th busiest road.
Black = 6th busiest road.

Exercise E

Draw a sketch of a road sign near your home, showing the places and names of the roads. Colour your sketch using the same colours as in Exercise D.

CH Exercise F

Look at the road signs above, and then copy and complete the sentences.

1. To get to Pickering, take the next road (left / right).
2. To get to York, take the next road (left / right).
3. The road to Newark is called the (A46 / A64).
4. Newark is (closer / further) than Leicester.
5. Newark is (closer / further) than Lincoln.

Exercise G

Make a list of places shown on road signs in your area. Do as many as you can. **Be careful! Remember your highway code.**

T Exercise H

On a map of your area, mark on as many places as you can from your list in Exercise G.

Exercise I

Copy and complete this chart:

Questions	Answers
Name your town or city Name your county Name the counties next to your county Name your region Name the most important town in your region Name something your region is famous for Name someone famous from your region.	

T Exercise J

On a map of your region, measure the distances between your home and **ten** other places.
Set your answers in a chart, like this. On your chart, write the real names of the places you have used.

Distance from my home	
Place 1	_____ miles
Place 2	_____ miles
Place 3	_____ miles
Place 4	_____ miles
Place 5	_____ miles
Place 6	_____ miles
Place 7	_____ miles
Place 8	_____ miles
Place 9	_____ miles
Place 10	_____ miles

Exercise K

1. Do you live in England, Scotland, Wales, Northern Ireland or the Republic of Ireland?
2. Is your capital city called London, Edinburgh, Cardiff, Belfast or Dublin?

Exercise L

Write **5** sentences about your country.

Acknowledgements

The publishers would like to thank the following people
for their permission to use copyright material:

Airviews p.22 bottom, 26;
BBC Enterprises p.46;
Daily Telegraph Colour Library p.18, 20, 21 both, 28 top
left, 66 bottom;
Robert Harding Picture Library p.28 bottom left and
right;
Holt Studios p.48 both;
Sealand Aerial Photography p.4 right, 27, 31;
South Wales Evening Post p.16, 32;
Simon Warner Photography p.28 centre left, 30, 34, 37,
39, 44 (all), 45, 49, 64 bottom left, 75, 78.